"Bring on the apps! Marissa's smart, stylish take is a celebration of how we love to eat today."

—**KERRY DIAMOND, founder of *Cherry Bombe Magazine***

"Marissa's beautiful book has completely shifted my perspective on appetizers from just a side focus to the full meal. Filled with thoughtful combinations, from flavors to full appetizer menus, this book is bursting with creative, delicious ideas, and I've already bookmarked (too) many!"

—**JUSTINE DOIRON, *New York Times* bestselling author of *Justine Snacks***

"As someone who arrives at every party ravenously hungry, delicious and satisfying apps are very important to me. I now have a new standard to hold all other apps to: Marissa has raised the bar with her new book."

—**DAN PELOSI (AKA GROSSYPELOSI), *New York Times* bestselling author of *Let's Party***

"There are no fussy garnishes or foams here—just simple formulas, tips, and tricks for how to feast with your eyes first. Whether it's a pinwheel appetizer or her specialty, a cheese plate, Marissa has made sure it's gorgeous, packed with flavor, and attainable for even the most timid of home cooks."

—**CAROLINE CHAMBERS, author of the Substack and *New York Times* bestseller *What to Cook When You Don't Feel Like Cooking***

"Marissa's cookbook is an invitation to relax and enjoy irresistible apps and satisfying sips while making cherished memories. She cleverly unlocks the secret to hosting through thoughtful yet effortless recipes everyone will love."

—**CAROLINA GELEN, *New York Times* bestselling and James Beard Award winning author of *Pass the Plate***

I'll Bring the Apps

I'll Bring the Apps

BITES, BOWLS,
BOARDS
& BEVERAGES

Marissa Mullen

PHOTOGRAPHS BY NICO SCHINCO

UNION SQUARE & CO.
NEW YORK

UNION SQUARE & CO.
NEW YORK

Union Square & Co.
Hachette Book Group
1290 Avenue of the Americas, New York, NY 10104
unionsquareandco.com
@unionsqandco

First Edition: March 2026

Union Square & Co. is an imprint of Grand Central Publishing, a division of Hachette Book Group, Inc. The Union Square & Co. name and logo are registered trademarks of Hachette Book Group, Inc.

Editor: Amanda Englander
Designer: Renée Bollier
Photographer: Nico Schinco
Food Stylist: Kaitlin Wayne
Prop Stylist: Maeve Sheridan
Production Editor: Ivy McFadden
Production Manager: Terence Campo
Copy Editor: Kerry Acker

Library of Congress Control Number: 2025943014

ISBNs: 978-1-4549-6117-8 (hardcover)
978-1-4549-6118-5 (e-book)

Printed in China

1010

10 9 8 7 6 5 4 3 2 1

To my parents, Jim and Ellen,
who taught me that even Tuesday nights
deserve delicious food, mood lighting,
and a themed playlist

CONTENTS

BOARDS 133

BEVERAGES 203

The Starting Course

Whether I'm the party host planning every meticulous detail, or a grateful guest lucky enough to simply show up, one thing remains constant: I'll always offer to bring the apps!

Appetizers are a simple reminder that the best moments often begin with small gestures. And they're arguably the best part of every meal. At any gathering, I naturally gravitate toward the snack table, which is consistently my favorite part of any meal or party—and for good reason. A great appetizer spread creates a memorable first impression. The dishes act as a warm welcome, and an invitation to sit back, relax, and stay awhile.

My love for appetizers is lifelong, but it accidentally became my calling when I left my job in the music business to create cheese plates full-time. Cheese plates, to me, are a form of self-care. In my previous cookbooks, *That Cheese Plate Will Change Your Life* and *That Cheese Plate Wants to Party*, I highlight my "Cheese by Numbers" method, which features the six essential (according to me) categories for building a balanced cheese plate: cheese, meat, produce, crunch, dip, and garnish. (You can read more about it on page 138 if you're not already familiar.) This approach encourages a sense of simplicity, taking the guesswork out of seemingly intimidating creations. The concept resonated with many, and I (also accidentally) triggered a cultural shift in the way we entertain with the rise of the charcuterie trend in 2020. I always loved hosting "cheese parties" in my New York City apartment, sharing elaborate creations with both friends and strangers. With cheese as the main course, these parties were a highlight of our social gatherings. After almost a decade of Brooklyn living, I came across a charming farmhouse and decided to make the move to the Hudson Valley. Life upstate is slower, feels much more intentional, and my days are full of new interactions. Dinner parties became my norm. With that, I of course still volunteer to make the cheese plate every time, but my palate and my recipes have expanded, incorporating flavors from local makers and a growing appreciation for what's in season.

I'll be honest with you, though—I really don't love cooking dinner. When I have guests over, I want to be present and engaged, not hiding away in the kitchen up to my eyeballs in pots and pans, only to emerge once I finally set dinner down on the table. A simple snacky party has always been my go-to. A gathering with casual apps allows for better flow and more space for activities, and it's an efficient way to host groups whether small or large.

Now, I can hear my mom saying, "Marissa, too many apps will ruin your appetite before dinner." Sorry, Mom—this is not the book for that. This book is for those who want to have a low-effort yet memorable gathering, with an array of snacks to set the scene. Of course, you can pick and choose from the appetizers in the book to complete a full menu from entrée to dessert, but I'm here to show you how to kick off the party in a calm and collected headspace.

Come Hungry, Stay Awhile

So how do we narrow down the wide world of appetizer options? In the kitchen I am always thinking about how to serve up a variety of flavors and textures. By adding some accompaniments to the beloved cheese plate, we can expand the table spread in a simple yet effective way. In this book, I've narrowed that down into four distinct categories: bites, bowls, boards, and beverages. (Conveniently, this approach also scratches my itch for alliteration.)

BITES

A bite is a small, handheld snack that doesn't require utensils. It's easy to pick up and enjoy with minimal mess, making it ideal for eating while mingling. Bites are curated for optimal flavor and texture, focusing on ingredients that pair well and complement each other. These can be skewers, crostini, meatballs, or anything that you can eat in a bite or two.

BOWLS

A bowl is a dish served family style, designed for group enjoyment. Bowls often feature scoopable foods, allowing guests to personalize their servings. Examples include dips, salads (both pasta and green), casseroles, and puddings.

BOARDS

A board is a creatively arranged assortment laid out on a flat surface, also designed for easy sharing. Boards offer a variety of flavors, textures, and colors. The charcuterie board is a classic, but sandwiches and even pizza can make up a board. All of the elements are curated to pair well with the others. For obvious reasons, boards are a favorite of mine!

BEVERAGES

The right drink pairing can really elevate an appetizer experience. Picture a fizzy spritz cutting through the taste of creamy mozzarella, or a dirty martini adding extra brine to accompany a roasted garlic dip. You always need something to wash down all that deliciousness!

The Essential Flavors

Sweet, salty, sour, bitter, and umami are the five basic tastes that make up the way we experience food. Together, they create balance and excitement on your palate. Sweet is the cozy warmth of sugar, like honey or a ripe peach in summer. Salty is the satisfying bite of sea salt on a potato chip, or the brine of an olive. Sour is the tang that wakes up your taste buds, like the zing of a lemon or vinegar. Bitter is complex and bold, like dark chocolate or a red radish, which adds bite to a dish. Last, umami is synonymous with savory, lending depth and making something like Parmigiano-Reggiano so memorable.

When I'm cooking or crafting a spread, I always start here and strive to create a sense of balance and harmony on the table. But sometimes, those foundational flavors need a little extra flair. Enter: creamy, fresh, caramelized, and zesty. You'll find me using these adjectives a lot throughout the book.

CREAMY

Whether a lush burrata or a whipped feta dip, notes of cream provide a smooth, milky, mild base to build upon. Even if you don't eat cheese or dairy, you can use something like coconut yogurt or cashew cheese as the base for your creamy texture.

FRESH

To balance the creamy and savory notes, we need something juicy and vegetal. This might be a leafy green salad, a juicy ripe heirloom tomato, or a cold, crunchy cucumber. Fresh produce tends to have a cleansing effect on the palate, helping to refresh your taste buds.

CARAMELIZED

Caramelization happens when sugars in food cook and transform, creating deep, rich, and slightly sweet flavors, which are a great contrast to salty and savory notes. Think slow-cooked onions or jammy roasted garlic.

ZESTY

Tangy, sour, and spicy notes can fall under the zesty category, and this is where we add a bit of zing to the meal. Something like a cornichon, grainy mustard, or pickled red onion can really brighten up a dish if you feel like something is missing.

APPS: An Acronym

Curating an appetizer spread is a combination of balance and personal preference. Bites, bowls, and boards can be combined interchangeably, but it's always helpful to consider the size of the group, layout of the tablescape, and variety of dishes you want to include. You'll see that for each recipe, I recommend two additional dishes to round out the flavors for a well-balanced menu. I've also put together some themed menu options at the end of the book, with suggestions for making full spreads. Of course, feel free to create your own pairings and have fun with it. If you want to serve up a pink Galentine's theme with the Swirled Roasted Beet Whipped Feta and Maple Carrots (page 75) and the Red Wine Poached Pears (page 64), the world is your oyster. There are no real rules here—it's all about personal preference!

I've always loved a good method. When you follow something structured yet flexible, creativity can feel effortless. Just as my Cheese by Numbers method broke down the art of cheese boards into an intuitive step-by-step process, I wanted to distill this idea of creating spreads into an easy-to-follow formula. The APPS method ensures that your party-hosting bases are covered, while still allowing room for personal style and spontaneity. From the lighting in your space to the pairings on your table, it's all about creating a balanced experience that feels true to you.

A

AMBIENCE: Consider the vibe you're going for. That includes light—if it's a daytime party, natural light is your friend. As the sun sets, opt for candles, table lamps, and/or standing lamps. I personally can't stand the big overhead light—it makes everything feel like a sterile hospital! Another nonnegotiable for me is music. Music can instantly transform a room, prompting memories and nostalgia. I love to blast an upbeat playlist for a summer pool party, full of early 2000's hits, or a soft folk playlist when gathering around a cozy fireplace.

P

PRESENTATION: We always eat with our eyes first, so table decor and food styling are crucial elements for hosting a party. I like to work with a cohesive mood board for my tablescape, pulling colors from the food itself for the florals and linens. As for styling, you can take inspiration from my Cheese by Numbers method to ensure your dishes are looking professional. Adding some finishing garnishes like edible flowers and herbs can also elevate a dish in a simple way.

P

PAIRINGS: Pairings can be complex—and that word tends to feel intimidating. I'm here to remind you that at the core, pairings are personal. You enjoy eating peanut butter cups with Manchego? Great! That said, I do have some pairing tips to help you get started. (page 19)

S

SPACE: The space of your setting determines how to set up your apps. What is the size of the gathering? Is it a brunch party, happy hour snacks, an evening game night, or a late-night hang? When you're hosting, the amount of people attending does determine how heavy you want the snacky bites to be and how much food to serve. Also, consider the placement of the apps table. I always make sure it's set in a place where guests can easily help themselves to the food and don't accidentally get stuck in the corner.

THE PAIRING PRACTICE

WHAT GROWS TOGETHER GOES TOGETHER Like pairing wine, this philosophy always leads me in the right direction. Fresh mozzarella and tomatoes are both staples of Italian cuisine and natural companions. Add a drizzle of Italian olive oil and a sprinkle of flaky salt, and you've got a combination that's been perfected over centuries.

CREATE YOUR OWN Ultimately at the end of the day, there are no *real* rules when it comes to pairings. Let your curiosity guide you. We all have personal preferences, and sometimes you just might not like something. That's totally okay! Play around, trust your instincts, and let each new discovery bring a little joy to your table.

OPPOSITES ATTRACT I'm always drawn to contrasts, like sweet and salty, savory and tangy, or creamy and fresh. The duality makes for a lovely sensory experience for the palate. Try pairing lush burrata with a fresh nectarine, or sweet Italian chicken sausage with tangy grainy mustard. If we expand outside of the individual flavor profiles, we can even find opposites to pair dishes themselves. A crisp green salad cuts through the decadence of a baked Brie, while a zucchini and potato fritter is a starchy, crispy complement to fresh cucumber bites.

FLAVOR FRIENDSHIP Similarities go a long way when it comes to pairings. Think of the sweet, earthy warmth of roasted butternut squash, and how it pairs wonderfully with a maple syrup glaze. Or the combination of lemony whipped feta served with pickled radishes, where the bitter notes of the radish complement the zesty cheese.

MEMORIES AND MUSINGS Food is associated with memory and nostalgia, which can greatly influence your choices when it comes to different pairings. Any time I dive into a bowl of cowboy caviar, I'm sent back to childhood at our family barbecues. With a memory, the bite in the present moment is much more satisfying.

BITES

A BITE, OR A SMALL, HANDHELD APPETIZER, is the ideal choice when you just want a taste of something delicious, without committing to a full meal. These are usually bursting with flavor, curated to capture the essence of multiple pairings within a small surface area. Bites can either be passed for snacking while standing, or served on a platter with the rest of your appetizer spread. Just be aware of the complexity and logistics of the bite—for example, a cucumber bite is easy to consume while standing, whereas a deviled egg might be easier to eat over a small plate or napkin.

Potato Pancakes

WITH A SMOKY TWIST

Whenever I meet someone new, I love to ask them, "What are your three favorite potato styles?" It's a fun way to break the ice and the answer can say so much about someone's tastes. For me, latkes, or potato pancakes, always make the list. I'm obsessed with their golden, crispy edges and soft interior, and they make a great slate for layering flavors. In this recipe, I've taken the classic latke and added a zucchini twist, creating a potato-zucchini fritter hybrid. The finishing touch is a cool, smoky chipotle sour cream that balances the savory richness with a hint of spice.

- 2 medium russet potatoes, peeled
- 1 medium zucchini
- 1 small yellow onion, finely chopped
- 2 large eggs, lightly beaten
- ½ cup all-purpose flour
- ½ teaspoon garlic powder
- ½ teaspoon kosher salt, plus more to taste
- ¼ teaspoon freshly ground black pepper
- 3 tablespoons vegetable oil, plus more as needed
- Flaky salt
- ½ cup full-fat sour cream
- 1 tablespoon finely chopped chipotle pepper in adobo sauce
- 1 teaspoon fresh lime juice
- Chopped fresh parsley, for serving

1. Using the large holes of a box grater, grate the potatoes and zucchini. Working in batches as needed, place the grated vegetables in a clean kitchen towel or cheesecloth and squeeze out all the liquid over the sink until as dry as possible. Transfer to a large bowl and add the onion, eggs, flour, garlic powder, salt, and black pepper. Stir to combine well.

2. In a large skillet, heat the vegetable oil over medium heat until shimmering. Scoop up 1 tablespoon of the potato-zucchini mixture and, using clean hands, gently pack it into a pancake. Place in the skillet. Repeat until the skillet is full of (but not crowded with) pancakes. Cook until golden brown on the bottom, 3 to 4 minutes, then use a spatula to flip and cook until golden brown on the other side, 3 to 4 minutes more. Transfer to

Recipe continues

NOTE: Place the drained and salted pancakes in a 200°F oven while you finish cooking the rest.

a paper towel–lined plate to drain and immediately sprinkle with flaky salt. Repeat with the remaining potato-zucchini mixture, adding more oil to the skillet between batches as needed.

3 Meanwhile, in a small bowl, stir together the sour cream, chipotle in adobo, lime juice, and a pinch of salt.

4 Arrange the pancakes on a platter, top each with a dollop of smoky sour cream, then sprinkle with flaky salt and chopped parsley. Serve immediately while warm.

Make It a Spread! *Serve alongside Charcuterie Cream Cheese (page 89) and Truffle Cheddar Breakfast Quesadillas (page 135).*

CHÈVRE, PROSCIUTTO, NECTARINES, HONEY, AND BASIL

RICOTTA, SMOKED SALMON, GREEN PEAS, LEMON, AND DILL

WHIPPED FETA, ROASTED RED PEPPERS, SALAMI, AND BALSAMIC GLAZE

CHEESE AND CROSTINI, THREE WAYS

EACH RECIPE MAKES 12 CROSTINI

One of my favorite classic appetizers is crostini. These crispy little toasts act as a blank canvas for all kinds of flavors, from fresh cheeses and savory charcuterie to vibrant herbs and crunchy finishes. What I love most is how crostini toppings can transport you to different settings through flavor alone. A chèvre, prosciutto, and nectarine combo reminds me of a sunny springtime picnic, while ricotta, smoked salmon, and dill takes me to a breezy coastal brunch. For a bold Mediterranean twist, whip up some feta with roasted peppers, salami, and balsamic glaze.

Crostini with Ricotta, Smoked Salmon, Green Peas, Lemon, and Dill

- ⅓ cup frozen green peas, thawed
- 1 teaspoon lemon zest
- Kosher salt and freshly ground black pepper
- ½ cup whole-milk ricotta cheese
- 2 teaspoons fresh lemon juice
- 3 sprigs dill, plus more for serving
- 12 crostini, homemade (recipe follows) or store-bought
- 6 thin slices smoked salmon, halved lengthwise
- Extra-virgin olive oil, for drizzling

Make It a Spread! *Serve alongside the Tarragon Egg Salad with Seeded Nutty Crumble (page 112) and Early Riser Plate (page 145).*

1 In a small bowl, combine the peas and lemon zest and season with salt and pepper. Use a fork to mash together until smooth.

2 In a food processor, combine the ricotta, lemon juice, and dill and season with salt and pepper. Process until smooth, 30 seconds. Taste and adjust the seasoning as needed.

3 Spread a layer of the ricotta mixture over each crostini, then top with a slice of smoked salmon followed by a small spoonful of mashed peas. Drizzle each crostini with olive oil and top with a sprinkle of dill and a pinch each of salt and pepper. Arrange on a platter and serve.

CROSTINI

MAKES 12 CROSTINI

1 baguette, cut into twelve ⅓-inch-thick slices
Extra-virgin olive oil
Flaky salt

1 Preheat the oven to 375°F.

2 Lightly brush both sides of each baguette slice with olive oil and arrange the slices on a baking sheet. Sprinkle with flaky salt. Bake for 8 to 10 minutes, flipping halfway through, until golden and crispy. Remove from the oven and let cool slightly before assembling.

Crostini with Chèvre, Prosciutto, Nectarines, Honey, and Basil

4 ounces chèvre, at room temperature

12 crostini, homemade (page 28) or store-bought

1 ripe nectarine, thinly sliced

2 tablespoons honey

6 slices prosciutto, torn

12 small fresh basil leaves

Freshly ground black pepper

Spread a layer of chèvre on each crostini, dividing evenly, then layer on two slices of nectarine and a drizzle of honey. Scrunch the prosciutto on top. Top each crostini with a fresh basil leaf and some pepper. Arrange on a platter and serve.

Make It a Spread! *Serve alongside the Spring Pea and Arugula Potato Salad (page 97) and Spring Fling Plate (page 139).*

A NOTE ON CHEESE PAIRINGS

For these crostini combos we're using three fresh cheeses: chèvre (goat cheese), ricotta (cow's-milk cheese), and whipped feta (sheep's-milk cheese). Each of these cheeses has its own distinct flavor that can be enhanced through contrasting or complementing tasting notes.

- **CHÈVRE:** Chèvre is a tangy and creamy goat cheese with notes of lemon and citrus. Complement these flavors with a fresh and slightly tart stone fruit like nectarine or apricot. Contrast with something salty like prosciutto or sweet like honey.
- **RICOTTA:** Ricotta is a milky, lush cow's-milk cheese with a subtle flavor profile. I like to enhance the creamy base with a zip of lemon or some herbaceous notes. Since the cheese itself is mild, we can build both salty and sweet pairings, like smoked salmon and green peas.
- **FETA:** Feta is a salty and briny sheep's-milk cheese with a subtle tang and crumbly texture. I love to double down on the brine here with salty salami and marinated roasted red peppers. Balsamic glaze acts as a nice contrast cutting through the salt with sweetness but still retaining a hint of vinegar tang.

Crostini with Whipped Feta, Roasted Red Peppers, Salami, and Balsamic Glaze

4 ounces feta cheese, lightly crumbled

¼ cup coarsely chopped roasted red peppers

2 tablespoons extra-virgin olive oil, plus more for drizzling

1 teaspoon fresh lemon juice

Freshly ground black pepper

12 crostini, homemade (page 28) or store-bought

6 thin slices salami, cut in half

Balsamic glaze, for drizzling

3 sprigs parsley, chopped, for serving

1 In a food processor, combine the feta, roasted red peppers, olive oil, and lemon juice and season with pepper. Process until the mixture forms a thick paste, about 1 minute.

2 Spread a layer of the whipped feta mixture over each crostini. Fold a slice of salami in half, then place it on top of the feta. Drizzle each crostini with balsamic glaze and olive oil and top with a pinch of parsley. Finish with a pinch of black pepper. Arrange on a platter and serve.

Make It a Spread! *Serve alongside the Creamy Eggplant Dip (page 81) and Spring Pea and Arugula Potato Salad (page 97).*

Chicken Sausage, Pepper, and Onion Bites

Chicken sausage is always a go-to ingredient when I don't feel like cooking. I slice it up, sauté for a few minutes, and have myself a juicy and flavorful snack. I love any recipe that is low-effort, high-reward, which is why this one is on heavy rotation in my household. Sweet Italian chicken sausage isn't as heavy as pork sausage, yet it still has those caramelized flavors that highlight the sweetness of the onion. Grainy mustard spices up the bite with some tang, all piled high on a fresh pepper for crunch.

MAKES 20 BITES

- 2 tablespoons extra-virgin olive oil
- 1 yellow onion, thinly sliced
- Kosher salt
- 1 teaspoon balsamic vinegar
- Freshly ground black pepper
- 3 links sweet Italian chicken sausage, cut into ¼-inch-thick slices
- 10 sweet mini peppers, halved lengthwise and seeded
- 3 tablespoons grainy mustard
- Chopped fresh chives, for serving

1 In a large skillet, heat the olive oil over medium heat until shimmering. Add the onion and a pinch of salt and cook, stirring occasionally, until softened and lightly browned, 6 to 8 minutes. Add the balsamic vinegar during the last 2 minutes of cooking. Season with salt and pepper to taste.

2 Add the chicken sausage to the onions and cook, stirring occasionally, until the chicken sausage is lightly browned and the onions have started to caramelize, 4 to 5 minutes.

3 Meanwhile, arrange the mini pepper halves on a platter, cut side up. Fill each pepper half with the sausage-onion mixture, dividing evenly. Top with a dollop of grainy mustard and sprinkle with chives. Serve immediately while warm.

Make It a Spread! *Serve alongside the Garlic Lover's Dip (page 80) and Buffalo Chicken Meatballs (page 38).*

Summer Shrimp Cups

Shrimp cocktail is a classic for a reason—and it has been one of my favorite appetizers for years. It's served cold, doesn't require an oven, and serves as a perfect light and fresh option before a big meal. This version adds a sweet and summery twist to the classic cocktail sauce, incorporating flavorful sweet mango and spicy chile sauce. Serve in a small cup for individual bites and even top with a paper umbrella for a festive twist!

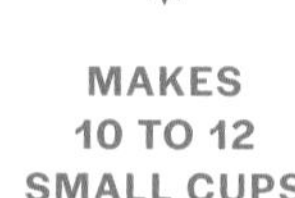

MAKES 10 TO 12 SMALL CUPS

- ½ cup diced (½-inch) peeled mango
- 2 teaspoons fresh lime juice
- 2 tablespoons rice vinegar
- 1 teaspoon honey
- 1 teaspoon chile paste
- ½ teaspoon grated fresh ginger
- 2 small garlic cloves, smashed
- 1½ teaspoons kosher salt, plus more to taste
- 1 lemon, sliced
- 1 teaspoon whole black peppercorns
- 1 pound raw extra-large shrimp, peeled (tails left on) and deveined
- 1 small bunch parsley, for serving

1. In a blender or food processor, combine the mango, lime juice, rice vinegar, honey, chile paste, ginger, a quarter of the smashed garlic, and ½ teaspoon salt. Puree on high speed until smooth, 45 seconds. Add water, 1 teaspoon at a time, if needed to reach your desired consistency. Transfer the mixture to a small bowl, cover, and chill in the refrigerator for at least 30 minutes.

2. Fill a large bowl with ice and water and set it nearby. In a large pot, combine 6 cups water, the lemon slices, the remaining smashed garlic, remaining 1 teaspoon salt, and the peppercorns. Bring the mixture to a gentle boil over medium-high heat, then reduce the heat to low and simmer. Add the shrimp and cook until pink and opaque, about 2 minutes. (Be careful not to overcook, as shrimp can become rubbery quickly!) Use a slotted spoon to transfer the cooked shrimp to the ice bath to cool for 5 minutes. Drain the shrimp and pat dry.

3. To serve, spoon ½ tablespoon chile sauce into a small cup, ramekin, or small plate. Add 2 shrimp, and sprinkle with fresh parsley. Repeat with the remaining shrimp.

Make It a Spread! *Serve alongside the Pineapple Cowboy Caviar (page 85) and Roast Beef Sliders with Emmental, Pickles, and Horseradish Crema (page 199).*

Tuna Tartare Bites

When tuna tartare makes an appearance at a party, the elegance factor automatically kicks up a notch. Something that might seem intimidating (raw fish) is actually so simple to prepare. Sushi-grade tuna has a clean, mild, and slightly sweet flavor with a silky, buttery texture. It's less "fishy" than many other types of raw fish, making it approachable even for those new to raw seafood. Soy sauce pairs well with raw tuna thanks to its salty, umami-rich flavor, and it enhances the fish without overpowering it. Ginger provides a refreshing, slightly sweet contrast that cleanses the palate between bites, while wasabi adds a bold zing that cuts through all the richness.

MAKES 20 BITES

8 ounces sushi-grade tuna, finely diced

1 tablespoon low-sodium soy sauce

1 tablespoon toasted sesame oil

1 tablespoon mayonnaise

1 tablespoon fresh lime juice

1 teaspoon grated fresh ginger

1 teaspoon rice vinegar

½ teaspoon wasabi paste

1 tablespoon finely chopped scallions

1 tablespoon sesame seeds

20 rice crackers (I like Ka-Me)

1 small avocado, diced

FOR SERVING

1 tablespoon microgreens

Flaky salt

Freshly ground black pepper

Red pepper flakes

1 In a medium bowl, combine the tuna with the soy sauce, sesame oil, mayonnaise, lime juice, ginger, and rice vinegar. Add the wasabi and gently stir well to combine. Stir in the scallions and sesame seeds.

2 Arrange the rice crackers on a serving tray or platter. Spoon a small amount of the tuna mixture onto each rice cracker and top each with a piece of avocado. Garnish with microgreens and sprinkle with flaky salt, black pepper, and red pepper flakes before serving.

Make It a Spread! *Serve alongside the Sweet Peach and Corn Salad (page 102) and Euro Summer Plate (page 153).*

Buffalo Chicken Meatballs

If you're like me and you only watch sports for the snacks, these Buffalo chicken meatballs will not disappoint. If you do like sports, well, here's another ball you can be a fan of. Meatballs make for a great single-serve bite and are simple to prep ahead of time. I like to cook them in the oven for an even bake, but if you're looking for a crispier exterior, you can finish them in a pan. This recipe hits the spot with the spicy Buffalo sauce, paired nicely with a cool and creamy blue cheese dip.

MAKES 24 MEATBALLS

- 1 pound ground chicken
- ⅓ cup plus 2½ tablespoons Buffalo sauce (I like Frank's RedHot)
- ⅓ cup panko breadcrumbs
- ¼ cup finely chopped celery
- ¼ cup finely chopped onion
- 1 large egg, lightly beaten
- 1 ounce blue cheese, crumbled
- 2 garlic cloves, minced
- 1 teaspoon kosher salt
- ½ teaspoon freshly ground black pepper
- ½ teaspoon smoked paprika
- ¼ cup blue cheese or ranch dressing
- Chopped fresh parsley, for serving
- Chopped fresh chives, for serving

Make It a Spread! *Serve alongside the Caramelized Onion Dip with Herbs (page 93) and Sausage, Pepper, and Onion Focaccia Pizza (page 190).*

1. Preheat the oven to 400°F. Line a baking sheet with parchment paper.
2. In a large bowl, combine the ground chicken, ⅓ cup of the Buffalo sauce, panko, celery, onion, egg, blue cheese crumbles, garlic, salt, pepper, and smoked paprika. Using clean hands, mix gently until just combined. Use a small scoop or your hands to form the mixture into 1½-inch meatballs—you should have about 24. Place them on the prepared baking sheet.
3. Bake the meatballs for 18 to 20 minutes, until firm to the touch and an instant-read thermometer inserted into one meatball reads 165°F.
4. Meanwhile, in a small serving bowl, stir together the blue cheese dressing with the remaining 2½ tablespoons Buffalo sauce.
5. Remove the meatballs from the oven and let cool for 5 minutes. Arrange on a serving platter and sprinkle with parsley and chives. Serve with toothpicks and the dipping sauce on the side.

TAJÍN-WATERMELON AND HALLOUMI
ZESTY FETA AND MELON

FRESH CHEESE SKEWERS, THREE WAYS

EACH MAKES 24 SKEWERS

During a recent trip to Italy, I fell in love with the tradition of aperitivo. It's a moment to gather, sip, and snack before dinner, taking time to enjoy the company around you. I try to channel this energy more now that I've left NYC for upstate. I love to invite friends over for bites on my patio, creating a little aperitivo tradition of my own, and skewers are one of my favorite ways to serve an assortment of flavors in a fun, handheld form.

Caprese with Salami Skewers

- 8 ounces fresh mini mozzarella balls
- 3 ounces sliced Italian dry salami (24 slices)
- 12 fresh basil leaves, sliced lengthwise
- 6 ounces cherry tomatoes
- Balsamic glaze, for drizzling
- Extra-virgin olive oil, for drizzling
- Flaky salt
- Freshly ground black pepper

1. Working with one at a time, thread 24 short skewers with a mozzarella ball, a folded salami slice, a basil leaf, a cherry tomato, and another mozzarella ball, in that order.
2. Arrange the skewers on a platter and generously drizzle with balsamic glaze and olive oil. Sprinkle with a pinch each of flaky salt and pepper before serving.

Make It a Spread! *Serve alongside the Creamy Peperoncini and Pickled Onion Potato Salad (page 111) and Euro Summer Plate (page 153).*

Tajín-Watermelon and Halloumi Skewers

1 (3-pound) watermelon, cut into 24 (1-inch) cubes

1 tablespoon Tajín seasoning

1 tablespoon extra-virgin olive oil

8 ounces Halloumi cheese, cut into 24 (1-inch) cubes

4 Persian cucumbers, cut into 24 (½-inch-thick) rounds

Zest of 1 lemon

Honey, for drizzling

Juice of ¼ lemon

1 Place the watermelon in a medium bowl. Sprinkle the Tajín evenly over the top and toss gently to coat.

2 In a medium nonstick skillet, heat the olive oil over medium heat until shimmering. Add the Halloumi and cook until golden brown all over, 1 to 2 minutes per side. Remove from the skillet and let cool slightly.

3 Working with one at a time, thread 24 short skewers with a watermelon cube, a piece of Halloumi, and a cucumber round, in that order.

4 Arrange the skewers on a serving platter and sprinkle with lemon zest, a drizzle of honey, and a squeeze of lemon juice before serving.

Make It a Spread! *Serve alongside the Summer Shrimp Cups (page 34) and Mozzarella and Chicken Sausage Summer Pasta Salad (page 118).*

Zesty Feta and Melon Skewers

- 1 small honeydew melon, seeded and scooped into 24 balls
- Leaves from 4 or 5 sprigs parsley, plus 2 teaspoons chopped fresh parsley
- 2 (8-ounce) blocks feta cheese, cut into 24 (3/4-inch) cubes
- 24 pitted Castelvetrano olives
- 6 tablespoons extra-virgin olive oil
- 4 teaspoons fresh lemon juice
- 1 tablespoon honey
- 2 teaspoons chopped fresh mint
- Kosher salt and freshly ground black pepper

1 Working with one at a time, thread 24 short skewers with a honeydew ball, a parsley leaf, a feta cube, and an olive, in that order.

2 In a small bowl, whisk together the olive oil, lemon juice, honey, mint, and chopped parsley. Season with salt and pepper.

3 Drizzle the dressing over the skewers just before serving.

Make It a Spread! *Serve alongside the White Bean Dip with Tapenade (page 82) and The Best Tuna Sandwiches (page 200).*

Cucumber Bites

WITH BOURSIN, SMOKED SALMON, LEMON ZEST, AND DILL

These bites remind me of an afternoon in London. After a long day of exploring the city, my friend and I stumbled upon an adorable tea-room with a perfect view of Big Ben. They served us delicious small sandwiches with smoked salmon, cream cheese, and cucumber. We spent the afternoon laughing, feasting on mini sandwiches galore, and drinking—you guessed it—warm tea. This is a timeless pairing with a light and refreshing crunch, great for serving at brunch or before a big meal. For this recipe, I brightened up the flavors with lemon zest and dill and omitted the bread to create a simple bite.

MAKES 16 BITES

- 1 large English cucumber
- 1 (5-ounce) package Garlic & Fine Herbs Boursin cheese
- 3 ounces smoked salmon, cut into 16 small pieces
- Zest and juice of ½ lemon
- 16 small sprigs dill
- Freshly ground black pepper

1. Evenly slice the cucumber into 16 rounds, about ½ inch thick. Pat the slices dry with a paper towel on both sides.

2. Spread a small dollop of Boursin cheese on top of each cucumber slice, followed by a piece of smoked salmon. Sprinkle with lemon zest and drizzle lemon juice over each bite. Top with dill and a pinch of pepper before serving on a platter.

Make It a Spread! *Serve alongside the Melon Ball Summer Salad (page 101) and Simple Shop Plate (page 159).*

Elevated Potato Chips

Chips can be fancy, too. This no-recipe recipe takes one of my favorite snack foods and enhances it with glorious cheese pairings. Something like a dollop of sweet fig jam adds just the right amount of fruity sweetness, creating a delightful play between salty and sweet flavors. To finish it off, consider fresh thyme to add a subtle herbal note that elevates the whole bite, bringing an extra layer of complexity. These combinations are just suggestions, but you can create your own bites with chips from the pantry and whatever cheese you have left over in the fridge. They're a great little snack that almost feels like a personal cheeseboard!

MAKES 24 BITES

- 1 (7.5-ounce) bag wavy sea salt kettle chips (I like Cape Cod; about 24 chips)
- 2 (6-ounce) wheels goat Brie cheese, cut into 24 equal slices
- 4 ounces fig jam
- Leaves from 3 sprigs thyme

Arrange whole chips on a platter. To each chip, add a slice of the Brie, a dollop of the jam, and some thyme leaves to finish. Serve immediately.

Make It a Spread! *Serve alongside the Citrus and Crunchy Green Salad with Fennel and Pomegranate (page 126) and The Best Tuna Sandwiches (page 200).*

VARIATIONS

Salt and Vinegar Chips with Blue Cheese: *The tangy chip combined with the pungent blue cheese reminds me of a dirty martini.*

Sour Cream and Onion Chips with Camembert: *The buttery Camembert complements the rich, savory notes of sour cream and onion chips.*

Jalapeño Chips with Aged Cheddar: *The spicy heat from the jalapeño chips brings out the deep, sharp flavors of aged cheddar, creating a fiery bite with a touch of smokiness.*

Handheld Pasta Salad

Think of these skewers as handheld pasta salad. Whether it's for a summer barbecue, a holiday party, or a casual gathering, these are easy to serve—no forks or even plates needed! I made this recipe as an appetizer for Thanksgiving a few years ago, and it was the ideal level of decadence—whetting our appetites without ruining them before the big meal. The skewering process is simple and repetitive, and if you put on a good podcast while you're doing it, it can be quite relaxing. You can also use festive toothpicks to set a party theme, like ones with snowflakes or disco balls—that's never not fun!

MAKES 24 SKEWERS

- 1 (9- to 12-ounce) package frozen cheese tortellini
- 3 tablespoons extra-virgin olive oil
- 1 tablespoon fresh lemon juice
- 2 teaspoons honey
- 1 teaspoon balsamic vinegar
- 1 garlic clove, minced
- ¼ teaspoon dried oregano
- Kosher salt and freshly ground black pepper
- 3 Persian cucumbers, cut into ¾-inch-thick slices
- 12 large fresh basil leaves, halved lengthwise
- 8 slices prosciutto, cut into thirds crosswise
- 24 pitted Castelvetrano olives
- 12 marinated artichoke hearts, halved lengthwise
- Balsamic glaze, for serving

1. Bring a medium pot of salted water to a boil over high heat. Add the tortellini and cook until al dente, 3 to 4 minutes. Drain and rinse with cool water to avoid sticking, then transfer to a large bowl.
2. Meanwhile, in a small bowl, whisk together the olive oil, lemon juice, honey, balsamic vinegar, garlic, and oregano until emulsified. Season with salt and pepper.
3. Add the cucumber to the bowl with the tortellini. Pour in the dressing and toss to coat well.
4. Working with one at a time, thread 24 skewers with a basil leaf slice, a tortellini, prosciutto, an olive, an artichoke heart half, a cucumber slice, and another tortellini, in that order.
5. Arrange the skewers on a serving platter. Sprinkle with pepper and finish with a drizzle of balsamic glaze for a touch of sweetness.

Make It a Spread! *Serve alongside the Sweet and Spicy Whipped Brie (page 86) and Citrus and Crunchy Green Salad with Fennel and Pomegranate (page 126).*

Cheesy Puff Pastry Pinwheels

These puff pastry pinwheels are a holiday entertaining favorite in my home. Not only are they easy to make, but they also create a cool, funky swirl design on your table. The combination of Brie, olives, and pepperoni takes me back to my childhood, when my dad would bring home cheesy pepperoni bread from the local Italian deli. These pinwheels are a nod to nostalgia, elevated with Gruyère and honey mustard to contrast the buttery puff pastry.

MAKES 12 PINWHEELS

- 1 (8.5-ounce) sheet puff pastry, thawed
- 2 tablespoons grainy mustard
- 2 tablespoons honey mustard
- 6 ounces Brie cheese, rind removed and sliced into cubes
- 3 ounces Gruyère cheese, shredded
- ¼ cup chopped pitted Castelvetrano olives
- ¼ cup chopped roasted red peppers
- ¼ cup diced pepperoni
- 2 teaspoons finely chopped fresh rosemary, plus more for serving

1. Preheat the oven to 400°F.
2. On a clean work surface, roll out the puff pastry into a 12-inch square. Spread a layer of grainy mustard and honey mustard over the puff pastry, edge to edge. Evenly scatter the Brie, Gruyère, olives, roasted red peppers, pepperoni, and rosemary on top.
3. Working from the edge closest to you, roll the puff pastry into a log shape, then slice it evenly into 12 pinwheels and arrange on a baking sheet, spacing them apart.
4. Bake the pinwheels for 12 to 15 minutes, until puffed and golden brown. Remove from the oven, sprinkle with more rosemary, and serve!

Make It a Spread! *Serve alongside the Chopped Brussels and Pecorino Salad (page 125) and Root Vegetable Soup Coupes (page 129).*

Savory Jammy Onion Toasts

A few winters ago, my friends and I rented a chalet in the Alps, right on the border between France and Switzerland. Nestled in the peaks of Mont Blanc, we spent our days playing in the snow, watching movies by the fire, and indulging in plenty of fondue. Just to the north of us lay the Jura Mountains, where Comté, the French fondue staple, was first crafted. Comté is one of France's most beloved cow's-milk cheeses, aged for several months to develop a rich, nutty, and slightly sweet flavor. Here, the savory ham, caramelized onion jam, and creamy cheese come together to create a delightful balance of flavor. These toasts transport me straight back to that cozy chalet.

MAKES 12 SMALL TOASTS

- 2 tablespoons unsalted butter
- 1 large yellow onion, thinly sliced
- Kosher salt and freshly ground black pepper
- 1 tablespoon light brown sugar
- 1 tablespoon balsamic vinegar
- 1 teaspoon fresh thyme leaves
- 1 garlic head
- 3 tablespoons extra-virgin olive oil
- 4 thick slices sourdough bread
- Flaky salt
- 4 slices deli ham
- 6 ounces Comté cheese
- Chopped fresh rosemary, for serving

1. Preheat the oven to 375°F.
2. In a medium skillet, melt the butter over medium heat. Add the onion and season with a pinch each of salt and pepper. Reduce the heat to medium-low and cook the onions slowly, stirring occasionally, until golden brown and caramelized, about 25 minutes. Stir in the brown sugar, balsamic vinegar, and thyme. Cook, stirring, until the liquid has reduced and coats the onions, 2 to 3 minutes more.
3. Meanwhile, slice the garlic head in half crosswise, brush cut sides with 1 tablespoon of the olive oil, place cut side up, and wrap in aluminum foil. Roast for 30 minutes, until soft and caramelized.
4. Using a sharp knife, cut the shorter ends off each sourdough slice, and cut into 3 even rectangles. Place on a baking sheet, lightly brush both sides with the remaining 2 tablespoons olive oil, and sprinkle with

Recipe continues

flaky salt. Bake for 8 to 10 minutes, flipping halfway through, until golden and crispy.

5 Meanwhile, slice the ham evenly into 12 rectangles, then slice the Comté evenly into 12 rectangles, about ⅓ inch thick.

6 Let the garlic cool for 10 minutes, then press to release the softened cloves and spread onto the top of each toasted sourdough slice, dividing evenly. Layer on the Comté, ham, and jammy onions. Return to the oven and broil for 3 to 5 minutes, until the cheese is melted. Top each slice with rosemary and serve.

Make It a Spread! *Serve alongside the Citrus and Crunchy Green Salad with Fennel and Pomegranate (page 126) and Fresh and Zesty Veggies (page 187).*

Veggie Meatballs

WITH CREAMY PESTO

These veggie meatballs are so hearty and flavorful, they'll make you appreciate just how satisfying vegetarian cooking can be. Here, we take finely chopped baby bellas and combine them with walnuts, onion, garlic, carrot, and zucchini to enhance each bite with texture and moisture. The Italian spices are reminiscent of a traditional meatball, while the Parmigiano-Reggiano adds salty and savory notes. The creamy pesto dipping sauce elevates with its basil-forward flavor, adding an herbaceous brightness. I make these to snack on weekly!

MAKES 16 MEATBALLS

MEATBALLS

1 tablespoon extra-virgin olive oil

8 ounces baby bella (cremini) mushrooms, finely chopped

1 small yellow onion, finely chopped

2 garlic cloves, minced

1 carrot, grated

1 zucchini, grated

Kosher salt and freshly ground black pepper

½ cup walnuts, finely chopped

1 cup Italian-style breadcrumbs

¼ cup freshly grated Parmigiano-Reggiano cheese

1 large egg

1 teaspoon dried oregano

1 teaspoon dried thyme

PESTO DIPPING SAUCE

¼ cup pesto

½ cup full-fat sour cream

1 teaspoon fresh lemon juice

1. **Make the meatballs:** Preheat the oven to 375°F. Line a baking sheet with parchment paper.
2. In a large skillet, heat the olive oil over medium heat until shimmering. Add the mushrooms, onion, garlic, carrot, and zucchini. Season with salt and pepper. Cook, stirring occasionally, until the vegetables are softened and lightly browned, 5 to 7 minutes. Transfer to a large bowl and add the walnuts, breadcrumbs, Parmigiano-Reggiano, egg, oregano, and thyme. Stir well to combine.
3. Using clean hands, form the mixture into 1½-inch balls—you should have about 16. Place them on the prepared baking sheet.
4. Bake the meatballs for 20 to 25 minutes, using a spatula to carefully flip them halfway through, until they are golden brown and firm.

Recipe continues

5 **Meanwhile, make the pesto dipping sauce:** In a small bowl, stir together the pesto, sour cream, and lemon juice until smooth. Season with salt and pepper.

6 Arrange the meatballs on a platter and serve warm, with toothpicks and the dipping sauce on the side.

Make It a Spread! *Serve alongside the Stuffed Mushroom Dip (page 69) and Chopped Brussels and Pecorino Salad (page 125).*

Maple-Candied Bacon Deviled Eggs

A deviled egg on a menu is an instant order for me, every time. I love the smooth, velvety filling with a hint of tangy mustard. With this recipe, I incorporated maple-candied bacon for a balance of smoky, savory, and sweet flavors. Beware of snacking on so much maple bacon that you run out of egg toppings (guilty). The rich yolk filling is a blend of mayo, mustard, maple syrup, and apple cider vinegar, making for a nice contrast to the salty, crispy bacon. These eggs are not just for brunch—serve them all through the fall, and at any time of day!

MAKES 12 DEVILED EGGS

---

4 bacon slices

2½ tablespoons maple syrup

1 tablespoon dark brown sugar

Freshly ground black pepper

6 large eggs

2 tablespoons mayonnaise

1 tablespoon Dijon mustard

1 teaspoon apple cider vinegar

Kosher salt

Smoked paprika, for serving

Chopped fresh chives, for serving

1 Preheat the oven to 375°F. Line a baking sheet with parchment paper or aluminum foil.

2 Place the bacon slices on the prepared baking sheet in a single layer. Brush the bacon slices with ½ tablespoon of maple syrup, dividing evenly, then sprinkle with brown sugar and ½ teaspoon pepper.

3 Bake the bacon for 15 to 20 minutes, until crispy and caramelized. Remove from the oven and transfer to a paper towel–lined plate to drain, cool, and crisp up. Crumble into small pieces.

4 Meanwhile, fill a large bowl with ice and water and set it nearby. Place the eggs in a medium saucepan and cover with water. Bring to a boil over high heat, then reduce the heat to low and cook for 12 minutes. Using a slotted spoon, transfer the eggs to the ice bath to cool. Carefully peel the eggs and slice them in half

Recipe continues

NOTE: To pipe, spoon the yolk mixture into a piping bag or a zip-top bag with one corner snipped off. Twist the top of the bag and gently squeeze to pipe the filling into each egg white half.

lengthwise. Transfer the yolks to a small bowl. Arrange the whites on a serving platter.

5 Add the mayonnaise, Dijon mustard, apple cider vinegar, and the remaining 2 tablespoons maple syrup to the yolks and season with salt and pepper. Use a fork to break up the yolks and mix until creamy and well combined.

6 Spoon or pipe the yolk mixture back into the egg whites and top each with a generous sprinkle of crumbled candied bacon, a dash of smoked paprika, and chives.

Make It a Spread! *Serve alongside the Maple Tofu and Squash Sandwiches (page 194) and Veggie Meatballs with Pesto (page 57).*

Red Wine Poached Pears

Presentation is key when it comes to making an impressive appetizer, and these poached pear halves will elevate any gathering. Their striking deep red hue actually inspired me to find more maroon for my wardrobe—I can't get enough of the color. The poaching process also brings out the natural sweetness of the pears, making them an ideal partner to the pungent blue cheese. As these aren't quite handheld bites, the pear becomes soft enough to seamlessly slice with a fork. It's the perfect moody winter centerpiece.

MAKES 8 HALVES

- 1 (750ml) bottle merlot
- ½ cup sugar
- 2 cinnamon sticks
- 4 whole cloves
- 2 strips of orange peel
- 2 teaspoons pure vanilla extract
- 4 firm Bosc pears, peeled, halved lengthwise, and cored
- 6 ounces blue cheese, crumbled
- 3 ounces walnuts, toasted
- 1 tablespoon honey, for drizzling

1. In a large pot, combine the merlot, sugar, cinnamon sticks, cloves, orange peel, and vanilla over medium heat. Cook, stirring, until the sugar dissolves, about 7 minutes. Add the pear halves to the poaching liquid, cut side down, ensuring they're mostly submerged. Reduce the heat to low and simmer until knife-tender, turning the pears halfway through if they're not fully submerged, 18 to 20 minutes. Remove the pot from the heat. Let the pears cool in the poaching liquid for at least 30 minutes to absorb more flavor. The longer they soak, the deeper the flavor becomes. You can even soak them overnight in the fridge!

2. Arrange the pears face up on a serving platter. Top each with blue cheese and toasted walnuts, dividing evenly. Drizzle with honey before serving.

NOTE: For a nonalcoholic version, place the halved pears cut side up on a baking sheet. Brush with honey and bake at 375°F for 25 minutes.

Make It a Spread! *Serve alongside the Burrata with Winter Citrus and Toasted Walnuts (page 107) and Root Vegetable Soup Coupes (page 129).*

BOWLS

BOWLS INVITE INTERACTION, encouraging guests to scoop, spread, and mix as they create their own ideal servings. I love bowls that have an artistic element, with vibrant colors of produce, herby garnishes, and olive oil swirls. Dips and salads are easy to make ahead of time and simple to transport, so they're the best dishes to bring to a gathering and serve at room temperature. As for presentation, I love to serve dips in shallow bowls with ample space to spread, while salads shine in large wooden or ceramic bowls. If you're in need of some fillers on the table, place small bowls of crackers, fresh bread, olives, spiced nuts, or cornichons.

Stuffed Mushroom Dip

This recipe takes everything I love about cheesy stuffed mushrooms and turns it into a dippable form. Be prepared for this dish to disappear first when serving it at a party. The satisfying combination of Boursin and cream cheese makes for a lush base, while the sautéed mushrooms, onions, garlic, and herbs add savory depth. Top with breadcrumbs and Parmigiano-Reggiano to create a nutty, golden crust during baking. Served warm, this dip is great for winter parties, game days, or cozy nights in.

SERVES 6 TO 8

- 2 (5-ounce) packages Garlic & Fine Herbs Boursin cheese, at room temperature
- 1 (8-ounce) package full-fat cream cheese, at room temperature
- ⅔ cup freshly shredded Parmigiano-Reggiano cheese, plus more for topping
- ¼ cup breadcrumbs, plus more for topping
- 3 tablespoons balsamic vinegar
- 2 tablespoons heavy cream
- 3 tablespoons extra-virgin olive oil
- 2 cups chopped baby bella (cremini) mushrooms
- 1 cup chopped yellow onion (about 1 medium onion)
- 3 garlic cloves, minced
- 2 teaspoons fresh thyme leaves, plus more for serving
- 2 teaspoons chopped fresh rosemary, plus more for serving
- Kosher salt and freshly ground black pepper
- Flatbread crackers, for serving

1 Position a rack in the top third of the oven and preheat to 350°F.

2 In a large bowl using a handheld mixer (or in the bowl of a stand mixer fitted with the paddle attachment), combine the Boursin, cream cheese, Parmigiano-Reggiano, breadcrumbs, balsamic vinegar, and cream and beat on medium speed until well combined and smooth, about 1 minute.

3 In a large skillet, heat the olive oil over medium heat until shimmering. Add the mushrooms and onion and cook, stirring occasionally, until the mushrooms are browned and the onion is soft and translucent, 6 to 8 minutes. Add the garlic, thyme, rosemary, and a pinch each of salt and pepper. Cook, stirring, until fragrant, 2 minutes more. Remove from the heat and fold the mushroom mixture into the cheese mixture. Transfer the dip to an 8-inch square baking dish. Sprinkle more Parmigiano-Reggiano and breadcrumbs on top—as much or as little as you like—to cover.

Recipe continues

Make It a Spread! *Serve alongside the Sweet Potato and Turkey Casserole (page 94) and Fresh and Zesty Veggies (page 187).*

4 Bake the dip for 15 minutes, until golden brown around the edges, then turn on the broiler and cook (watching closely!) until the top is golden and bubbling, about 3 minutes more.

5 Sprinkle with fresh thyme and rosemary. Serve warm with flatbread crackers alongside.

WHIPPED HERBY
LEMON FETA

SWIRLED ROASTED BEET WHIPPED FETA AND MAPLE CARROTS

WHIPPED FETA, TWO WAYS

✸

EACH SERVES
4 TO 6

Feta has a distinct briny flavor profile with a tender yet crumbly texture. When whipped with Greek yogurt, the cheese morphs into a fluffy, luxurious spread that makes a great base for building flavor. Here, whipped feta takes on two personalities. One is a bright and fresh combination for spring, while the other is a warm and earthy nod to autumn.

Swirled Roasted Beet Whipped Feta and Maple Carrots

1 small garlic head

4 tablespoons extra-virgin olive oil, plus more for drizzling

2 medium carrots, coarsely chopped

1½ tablespoons maple syrup

Kosher salt and freshly ground black pepper

4 small red beets, chopped

8 ounces feta cheese

3 tablespoons plain full-fat Greek yogurt

¼ teaspoon smoked paprika

1 tablespoon fresh lemon juice

Flaky salt

Torn sourdough bread, for serving

1 Preheat the oven to 400°F.

2 Halve the garlic head crosswise, brush the cut sides with 1 tablespoon of the olive oil, place cut side up, and wrap in foil. Roast for 30 minutes, until soft.

3 Meanwhile, in a small bowl, toss the carrots with 1 tablespoon each of the olive oil and maple syrup. Season with salt and pepper. Arrange evenly on half of a baking sheet. In the same bowl, toss the beets with 1 tablespoon of the olive oil. Arrange on the other half of the pan. Roast alongside the garlic for 20 to 25 minutes, tossing halfway through, until caramelized. Remove from the oven and let cool.

4 In a food processor, add half the feta, half the yogurt, squeeze out the garlic cloves from their skins, add the roasted carrots, remaining ½ tablespoon maple syrup, ½ tablespoon of the olive oil, the smoked paprika, and a pinch each of salt and pepper. Process until smooth and creamy, about 1 minute. Season with more salt and pepper to taste. Spoon the carrot mixture into the bottom of a small shallow bowl.

5 Wipe out the bowl of the food processor. In the food processor, combine the remaining feta, remaining yogurt, the cooked beets, the remaining ½ tablespoon olive oil, the lemon juice, and a pinch each of salt and pepper. Process until smooth and creamy, about 30 seconds. Season with more salt and pepper to taste.

6 Dollop the beet mixture over the carrot mixture. Use a spatula to gently swirl the two together, creating a marbled effect but stopping short of fully mixing. Finish with a drizzle of olive oil and some flaky salt and pepper. Serve with torn sourdough alongside.

Make It a Spread! *Serve alongside the Autumn Harvest Cobb Salad (page 122) and Root Vegetable Soup Coupes (page 129).*

Whipped Herby Lemon Feta

WITH MARINATED RADISHES AND PEAS

8 ounces feta cheese, crumbled

½ cup plain full-fat Greek yogurt

2 tablespoons extra-virgin olive oil, plus more for drizzling

Zest of 1 lemon, plus more for serving

1½ tablespoons fresh lemon juice

2½ teaspoons honey

1 garlic clove, minced

1 tablespoon chopped fresh dill, plus more for serving

1 tablespoon chopped fresh chives, plus more for serving

½ cup Quick Pickled Radishes (recipe follows)

½ cup frozen green peas, thawed

Freshly ground black pepper

Warm pita bread, for serving

1 In a food processor, combine the feta, yogurt, olive oil, lemon zest, lemon juice, honey, garlic, dill, and chives. Process until smooth and creamy, 30 seconds. Transfer to a serving bowl and smooth the top.

2 Spoon the marinated radishes over the whipped feta. Scatter the green peas on top. Finish with more lemon zest, a drizzle of olive oil, a twist of black pepper, and additional dill and chives. Serve with warm pita bread alongside for dipping.

Make It a Spread! *Serve alongside the Cucumber Bites with Boursin, Smoked Salmon, Lemon Zest, and Dill (page 46) and Tarragon Egg Salad with Seeded Nutty Crumble (page 112).*

NOTE: The quick-pickle recipe can also be used to pickle sliced red onion, cucumber, or carrots; just sub the vegetable of your choice for the radishes. The longer the vegetables are refrigerated, the stronger the pickle flavor becomes.

QUICK PICKLED RADISHES

MAKES ABOUT 1 CUP

½ cup distilled white vinegar

1 tablespoon sugar

1 teaspoon sea salt

5 small red radishes, or 1 medium watermelon radish, thinly sliced into matchsticks

1 teaspoon mixed whole peppercorns

1 teaspoon mustard seeds

1 In a small saucepan, combine ½ cup water, the vinegar, sugar, and salt. Cook over medium heat, stirring, until the sugar and salt have dissolved, about 1 minute.

2 Place the sliced radishes in a clean large jar. Pour the hot brine over the radishes, ensuring they are fully submerged. Add the peppercorns and mustard seeds. Let the jar cool to room temperature, then seal the jar and refrigerate for at least 1 hour to let the flavors meld. The pickles will keep, refrigerated, for 2 to 3 weeks.

CREAMY
EGGPLANT DIP

GARLIC LOVER'S
DIP

WHITE BEAN DIP
WITH TAPENADE

ROASTED GARLIC DIP, THREE WAYS

✸

EACH SERVES
6 TO 8

I'll admit: I am a garlic girl. I love to load up my dishes with garlic goodness for that fragrant intensity. Roasted garlic is guaranteed to make your kitchen smell like a dream, and although it might not be the best option for first dates, it's a solid backbone for memorable appetizers. When paired with white beans, garlic adds complexity and depth. With roasted eggplant, it complements the smoky and savory notes. Add some garlic to lemon and herbs, and you have the perfect balance of zest and fresh flavors. These three roasted garlic dips are some of my favorite apps to bring to a dinner party or potluck, and generally just great dips to have up your sleeve.

Garlic Lover's Dip

2 garlic heads

½ cup extra-virgin olive oil, plus more for drizzling

1 cup plain full-fat Greek yogurt

1 tablespoon fresh lemon juice, plus more for serving

1 teaspoon onion powder

½ teaspoon red pepper flakes

2 tablespoons chopped fresh dill, plus more for serving

1 tablespoon chopped fresh parsley

4 scallions, finely chopped, plus more for serving

Kosher salt and freshly ground black pepper

Warm sourdough bread or potato chips, for serving

1 Preheat oven to 400°F.

2 Slice the garlic heads in half crosswise and brush the cut sides with 1 tablespoon of the olive oil, place cut side up, and wrap in aluminum foil. Roast for 30 minutes, until soft and caramelized. Let cool for 10 minutes, then squeeze the roasted garlic cloves out of their skins into a food processor.

3 Add the remaining ¼ cup olive oil, the yogurt, lemon juice, onion powder, and red pepper flakes and process until smooth, about 30 seconds. Add the dill, parsley, and scallions and pulse to combine. Season with salt and pepper.

4 Transfer the dip to a serving bowl and top with additional dill, scallions, a drizzle of olive oil, and a squeeze of lemon juice. Serve with warm bread or potato chips alongside.

Make It a Spread! *Serve alongside the Veggie Meatballs with Pesto (page 57) and Elevated Potato Chips (page 49).*

Creamy Eggplant Dip

2 globe eggplants

4 tablespoons extra-virgin olive oil, plus more for drizzling

1 garlic head

¼ cup plain full-fat Greek yogurt

2 tablespoons tahini

2 tablespoons chopped fresh parsley, plus more for serving

1 tablespoon chopped fresh dill, plus more for serving

2 teaspoons honey

1 tablespoon fresh lemon juice

½ teaspoon smoked paprika

¼ teaspoon onion powder

Kosher salt and freshly ground black pepper

Flaky salt

Pita chips, cucumber slices, and/or sourdough bread, for serving

1 Preheat the oven to 425°F.

2 Use a fork to poke several holes all over the skin of the eggplants, then slice them in half lengthwise. Brush the cut side of each half with ½ tablespoon of the olive oil and place them cut side down on a baking sheet. Slice the garlic head in half crosswise, brush the cut sides with 1 tablespoon of the olive oil, place cut side up, and wrap in aluminum foil. Place the eggplant and garlic in the oven and roast for 35 to 40 minutes, until the eggplant is tender and the garlic is browned and soft. Remove from the oven and let both cool for about 10 minutes.

3 Scoop out the flesh of the eggplants and place it in a food processor. Squeeze the roasted garlic cloves out of their skins into the food processor. Add the remaining 1 tablespoon olive oil, the yogurt, tahini, parsley, dill, honey, lemon juice, smoked paprika, and onion powder. Process until well combined, about 1 minute. Season with salt and pepper.

4 Spoon the dip into a shallow bowl and sprinkle with parsley, dill, and flaky salt. Drizzle with olive oil. Serve with pita chips, cucumber slices, or sourdough bread alongside.

NOTE: For a finishing touch that elevates both presentation and flavor, use the back of a spoon to create a gentle swirl across the surface of the dip. Drizzle olive oil into the grooves of the swirl, letting it pool slightly, and sprinkle with a pinch of flaky salt. Finally, scatter some fresh herbs on top for a pop of color.

Make It a Spread! *Serve alongside the Herby Feta and Grilled Chicken Pasta Salad (page 119) and Zesty Feta and Melon Skewers (page 45).*

White Bean Dip with Tapenade

1 garlic head

5 tablespoons extra-virgin olive oil, plus more for drizzling

1 (15-ounce) can cannellini beans, drained and rinsed

2 tablespoons fresh lemon juice

2 tablespoons chopped fresh rosemary, plus more for serving

½ teaspoon smoked paprika

½ teaspoon ground cumin

Kosher salt and freshly ground black pepper

⅓ cup pitted kalamata olives

1 tablespoon capers, drained and rinsed

1 garlic clove, minced

Pita chips, for serving

1 Preheat the oven to 400°F.

2 Slice the garlic head in half crosswise, brush the cut sides with 1 tablespoon of the olive oil, place cut side up, and wrap in aluminum foil. Roast for 30 minutes, until soft and caramelized. Let cool for 10 minutes, then squeeze the roasted garlic cloves out of their skins into a food processor. Add the cannellini beans, 1 tablespoon of the lemon juice, the rosemary, 2 tablespoons of the olive oil, the smoked paprika, and the cumin and process until smooth, about 1 minute. Season with salt and pepper. Transfer the white bean dip to a serving bowl and smooth out the top.

3 Wipe out the bowl of the food processor. In the food processor, combine the olives, capers, minced garlic, remaining 1 tablespoon lemon juice, and remaining 2 tablespoons olive oil. Pulse a few times until the mixture is finely chopped.

4 Spoon the olive mixture over the white bean dip and gently swirl it into the dip for a marbled effect. Drizzle all over with a bit more olive oil and top with fresh rosemary. Serve with pita chips alongside for dipping.

Make It a Spread! *Serve alongside the Zesty Feta and Melon Skewers (page 45) and Euro Summer Plate (page 153).*

Pineapple Cowboy Caviar

No barbecue is complete without this fresh and tangy bean and corn combination, also known as cowboy caviar. This Texas-born favorite found its way into my New England childhood kitchen every summer, where my mom put her own spin on the loaded dip. Black beans provide an earthy foundation, brightened by the fresh crunch of cucumber, corn, and bell pepper. The pineapple's tropical sweetness contrasts the jalapeño's heat, while red onion and cilantro add aromatic notes. Slicing and dicing the produce is the hardest part of the job here, but the effort is well worth the result. Pair it with tortilla chips for a hit of salty, crunchy texture.

SERVES 6 TO 8

- 1 (15-ounce) can black beans, drained and rinsed
- 1 (15-ounce) can corn kernels, drained
- 1 cup diced fresh pineapple
- 1 cup diced Persian cucumber (about 3)
- ½ cup diced red bell pepper
- ⅓ cup finely diced red onion
- ¼ cup chopped fresh cilantro
- 1 jalapeño, seeded and finely diced
- 2 tablespoons extra-virgin olive oil
- 2 tablespoons fresh lime juice
- 1 tablespoon apple cider vinegar
- 1 teaspoon honey
- 1 teaspoon ground cumin
- Kosher salt and freshly ground black pepper
- Tortilla chips, for serving

1 In a large bowl, combine the black beans, corn, pineapple, cucumber, bell pepper, red onion, cilantro, and jalapeño. Stir gently.

2 In a small bowl, whisk together the olive oil, lime juice, apple cider vinegar, honey, cumin, and a pinch each of salt and pepper.

3 Pour the dressing over the bean-corn mixture and toss to coat evenly. Season with more salt and pepper to taste.

4 Cover and refrigerate for at least 30 minutes before serving to allow the flavors to meld. Serve with tortilla chips alongside for scooping.

Make It a Spread! *Serve alongside the Summer Shrimp Cups (page 34) and Mozzarella and Chicken Sausage Summer Pasta Salad (page 118).*

Sweet and Spicy Whipped Brie

Did you know that Brie cheese can be whipped into a smooth, buttery, spreadable dip? This is one of my favorite ways to serve the French classic, although I'm not sure the French would approve of this non-traditional method (I apologize). For a sweet and spicy element, I like to use a bright red pepper jelly—one of those underrated spreads. I add crushed pistachios for a crunchy texture, and pomegranate seeds for sweet and tart notes. Serve at room temperature for a no-fuss app that guests will eagerly snatch up from your festive table.

SERVES 4 TO 6

---

2 (8-ounce) wheels Brie cheese

1 cup red pepper jelly

⅓ cup chopped shelled salted pistachios

¼ cup pomegranate seeds

Flatbread crackers, for serving

1 While the Brie is still cold from the fridge, use a knife or vegetable peeler to remove the rind from each wheel. Dice the cheese into cubes and place in a food processor. Let stand until the Brie warms to room temperature, then process until smooth and spreadable, 3 to 4 minutes. Transfer the whipped cheese to a shallow bowl (6 to 8 inches in diameter) and spread to cover the bottom.

2 Add the red pepper jelly on top of the cheese to cover. Sprinkle the pistachios all over the jelly, followed by the pomegranate seeds. Serve the dip at room temperature, with flatbread crackers.

Make It a Spread! *Serve alongside the Citrus and Crunchy Green Salad with Fennel and Pomegranate (page 126) and Handheld Pasta Salad (page 50).*

Charcuterie Cream Cheese

When you grow up in the tristate area, bagels are a big deal. Every bagel shop in my hometown has its own unique baking style, with a plethora of accompanying cream cheese flavors to pile high. Lox spread, cream cheese with scallions, and cream cheese flecked with veggies are ubiquitous, while more inventive flavors, like jalapeño or garlic and herb, are harder to find. Although I've had my fair share of bagels over the past few decades, I've never once come across a cream cheese with salami . . . until now. I call it charcuterie cream cheese. This decadent spread is full of salty and savory notes, from the chopped Castelvetrano olives to roasted red peppers, and the smoky salami to tie it all together. Fold in fresh chives for a bright, herbaceous flavor, and pair with bagel chips for dipping—or spread it straight over your favorite bagel.

SERVES 4 TO 6

---

8 ounces whipped cream cheese, at room temperature

4 ounces salami, diced

¼ cup diced roasted red peppers

¼ cup diced pitted Castelvetrano olives

2 tablespoons chopped fresh chives

Freshly ground black pepper

FOR SERVING

Chopped fresh dill

Sliced cucumbers

Cherry tomatoes on the vine

Bagel chips

1 In a medium bowl, combine the cream cheese, salami, roasted red peppers, olives, and chives and season with pepper. Stir well to combine.

2 Transfer the dip to a serving bowl and sprinkle with dill. Serve with cucumbers, cherry tomatoes, and/or bagel chips.

Make It a Spread! *Serve alongside the Early Riser Plate (page 145) and Melon Ball Summer Salad (page 101).*

Pumpkin Pie Dip

On Thanksgiving, my aunt always makes a plethora of pies. My favorite is the pumpkin, and I crave it all year long. This appetizer transforms the classic pumpkin pie into a dippable form. The mascarpone and cream cheese create a fluffy and luscious texture, while the pumpkin puree with cinnamon, nutmeg, and a touch of ginger brings a cozy warmth. Sprinkle the graham cracker crumble generously over the top for texture. I love to serve this dip with fresh sliced apples for seasonal crunch.

SERVES 4 TO 6

- 6 ounces mascarpone cheese, at room temperature
- 3 ounces full-fat cream cheese, at room temperature
- ½ (15-ounce) can pure pumpkin puree
- ¾ teaspoon ground cinnamon
- ½ teaspoon ground nutmeg
- ½ teaspoon ground ginger
- 1 tablespoon honey
- 2 tablespoons salted butter
- 4 graham crackers, crumbled
- 2 tablespoons dark brown sugar
- Apple slices, for serving

1. In a medium bowl using a handheld mixer (or in the bowl of a stand mixer fitted with the paddle attachment), combine the mascarpone and cream cheese. Beat on medium speed until smooth and fluffy, about 45 seconds. Add the pumpkin, ½ teaspoon of the cinnamon, the nutmeg, ginger, and honey and beat to combine.

2. In a medium skillet over medium heat, melt the butter. Add the graham crackers, brown sugar, and the remaining ¼ teaspoon cinnamon and stir to combine. Cook the graham cracker mixture until lightly browned and fragrant, about 5 minutes.

3. Spoon the dip into a serving bowl and top with the toasted graham cracker crumble. Serve with apple slices alongside.

Make It a Spread! *Serve alongside the Red Wine Poached Pears (page 64) and Chopped Brussels and Pecorino Salad (page 125).*

Caramelized Onion Dip with Herbs

Nothing hypes me up more than walking into a party and seeing a big bowl of sour cream and onion dip. The creamy and slightly sweet dip paired with a crunchy, salty chip is the type of combination that instantly brings you back for seconds. My dad often makes this version at family parties, which is a play on an Ina Garten classic. I decided to add my own twist with a variety of herbs to brighten up the sweet jammy onions. Not only is this recipe highly addicting, it's also simple to make!

SERVES 8 TO 10

- 2 tablespoons unsalted butter
- 2 large yellow onions, thinly sliced
- ½ teaspoon kosher salt
- ½ teaspoon sugar
- 1 teaspoon balsamic vinegar
- 1½ cups full-fat sour cream
- ½ cup mayonnaise
- ⅓ teaspoon garlic powder
- ⅓ teaspoon onion powder
- Freshly ground black pepper
- ¼ cup chopped fresh chives, plus more for serving
- 2 scallions, thinly sliced, plus more for serving
- 2 tablespoons chopped fresh dill, plus more for serving
- Potato chips, for serving

Make It a Spread! *Serve alongside the Buffalo Chicken Meatballs (page 38) and Sausage, Pepper, and Onion Focaccia Pizza (page 190).*

1. In a large skillet, melt the butter over medium heat. Add the onions and ¼ teaspoon of the salt. Cook, stirring occasionally, until the onions are browned and supersoft and jammy, 20 to 25 minutes. Add the sugar and balsamic vinegar during the last 5 minutes of cooking. Remove from the heat and let cool for 10 minutes.
2. In a medium bowl, combine the sour cream, mayonnaise, garlic powder, onion powder, and remaining ¼ teaspoon salt and season with pepper. Stir until smooth. When the onions have cooled, coarsely chop and fold them into the sour cream mixture. Stir in the chives, scallions, and dill. Cover and refrigerate the dip for at least 1 hour before serving to allow the flavors to meld.
3. Transfer the dip to a serving bowl and finish with pepper and additional chives, scallions, and dill. Serve with potato chips alongside for dipping.

Sweet Potato and Turkey Casserole

This casserole can be an appetizer, a side dish, or even a full-on meal—the choice is yours. I like to have this on the table when I know people might be on the hungrier side but I don't want to cook an entire elaborate dinner. The sweet potato, kale, and ground turkey are a glorious trifecta of sweet, bitter, and satiating flavors. Plus, I adore Gruyère melted over almost anything—its nutty sharpness comes through in every bite—and the crispy panko crust makes it a warm and cozy classic.

SERVES 6 TO 8

- Nonstick cooking spray
- 1½ tablespoons extra-virgin olive oil
- 1 pound 93% lean ground turkey
- 1 teaspoon smoked paprika
- Kosher salt and freshly ground black pepper
- 1 medium yellow onion, thinly sliced
- 2 garlic cloves, minced
- 2 small bunches kale, leaves stemmed and coarsely chopped
- 2 large sweet potatoes, peeled and thinly sliced
- 6 ounces Gruyère cheese, shredded
- ¾ cup whole milk
- ½ teaspoon ground nutmeg
- ½ cup panko breadcrumbs
- 2 tablespoons freshly grated Parmigiano-Reggiano cheese
- 1 tablespoon unsalted butter, melted

1 Preheat the oven to 375°F. Coat a 7 × 11-inch baking dish with cooking spray.

2 In a large skillet, heat 1 tablespoon of the olive oil over medium heat until the oil is shimmering. Add the turkey and ½ teaspoon of the smoked paprika. Season with salt and pepper. Cook, breaking up the meat with a wooden spoon, until cooked through and no longer pink, 6 to 8 minutes. Transfer to a bowl.

3 In the same skillet, heat the remaining ½ tablespoon olive oil over medium heat. Add the onion and garlic and cook, stirring occasionally, until the onion is soft and the garlic is fragrant, about 3 minutes. Add the kale, season with salt, and cook, stirring, until wilted, 3 minutes more. Transfer to a separate bowl.

4 Layer half the sweet potato slices in the bottom of the prepared baking dish. Sprinkle with the remaining

Recipe continues

Make It a Spread! *Serve alongside the Citrus and Crunchy Green Salad with Fennel and Pomegranate (page 126) and Root Vegetable Soup Coupes (page 129).*

½ teaspoon smoked paprika and season with salt and pepper. Spread half the cooked turkey over the sweet potatoes, followed by half the kale mixture, then half of the Gruyère. Repeat these layers with the remaining sweet potatoes, turkey, kale, and cheese.

5 In a small bowl, whisk together the milk, nutmeg, and a pinch each of salt and pepper. Pour the mixture evenly over the casserole. In the same small bowl, stir together the panko, Parmigiano-Reggiano, and butter. Sprinkle the mixture evenly over the top of the casserole.

6 Cover the casserole with aluminum foil and bake for 30 minutes. Remove the foil and bake for 10 to 15 minutes more, until the sweet potatoes are tender and the top is golden brown.

7 Remove and let cool for about 5 minutes before serving.

Spring Pea and Arugula Potato Salad

The key to this salad is a ricotta lemon dressing, one of my go-tos all season long—and a bright way to welcome the season. I first created this dressing for a pasta salad, and I loved it so much that it's become a staple in my repertoire. Now it's making a return alongside spring produce. The salad itself features some seasonal favorites, like asparagus, radishes, and arugula, with peas for a hint of sweetness, plus scallions and a mix of herbs. The potatoes add a smooth, starchy element, creating a satisfyingly hearty bowl to serve at your garden parties. If you like, try adding a poached egg on top of each plateful right before serving for a warm richness that contrasts the cool and crunchy greens.

SERVES 4 TO 6

---

4 to 6 asparagus spears, trimmed

5 or 6 baby potatoes, cubed

½ cup whole-milk ricotta cheese

2½ tablespoons fresh lemon juice

3 tablespoons extra-virgin olive oil

¼ cup plus 3 tablespoons chopped fresh basil

1 small shallot, minced

1 teaspoon honey

Kosher salt and freshly ground black pepper

3 cups arugula

½ cup frozen peas, thawed

6 radishes, thinly sliced into matchsticks

2 scallions, thinly sliced

¼ cup chopped fresh parsley

¼ cup chopped fresh dill

1. Fill a large bowl with ice and water and set it nearby. Bring a medium pot of salted water to a boil over high heat. Add the asparagus and cook until bright green and firm-tender, 2 to 3 minutes, then use tongs or a slotted spoon to transfer to the ice bath to cool. Drain and pat dry, then thinly slice. You should have about ½ cup.

2. Return the pot of water to a boil. Add the potatoes and cook until tender, 10 to 14 minutes. Drain and let cool slightly.

3. Meanwhile, in a small bowl, whisk together the ricotta, lemon juice, olive oil, 3 tablespoons of the basil, the shallot, and the honey. Season with salt and pepper.

4. When the potatoes are cool, place them in a large bowl along with the arugula, asparagus, peas, radishes,

Recipe continues

NOTE: For more zing, you can also add some Quick Pickled Radishes (page 77)!

scallions, parsley, dill, and remaining ¼ cup basil. Drizzle the ricotta dressing over the top and toss gently to coat. Season with additional salt and pepper to taste.

5 Serve immediately or chill for up to 30 minutes before serving.

Make It a Spread! *Serve alongside the Crostini with Chèvre, Prosciutto, Nectarines, Honey, and Basil (page 30) and The Best Tuna Sandwiches (page 200).*

Melon Ball Summer Salad

Picture this: You're enjoying time by a pool, lake, or ocean on a hot, sunny day. Then, someone opens a cooler and pulls out the answer to every summer craving: a refreshing melon and cucumber salad. This "salad" skips the lettuce to make a colorful, sweet, and juicy appetizer or side dish. Using a melon baller (or a knife for a dice, if you prefer), scoop out the trifecta of honeydew, watermelon, and cantaloupe with fresh cucumber and red onion. The dressing is a creamy green goddess blend to cut the punch of the onion while adding to the cool, smooth texture of the salad overall. The result is a dish that's as hydrating as it is flavorful.

SERVES 4 TO 6

- ½ ripe avocado
- 3 tablespoons extra-virgin olive oil
- 2 tablespoons fresh lemon juice
- 1 tablespoon honey
- 2 tablespoons chopped fresh basil, plus more for serving
- 2 tablespoons chopped fresh parsley, plus more for serving
- 1 tablespoon chopped fresh mint, plus more for serving
- Kosher salt and freshly ground black pepper
- ½ small honeydew melon, seeded and scooped into balls
- ½ small watermelon, seeded and scooped into balls
- ½ small cantaloupe, seeded and scooped into balls
- 1 cup cubed peeled cucumber
- ⅓ small red onion, thinly sliced
- ¼ cup shelled pistachios, toasted and finely chopped
- Flaky salt, for serving

1. In a blender or food processor, combine the avocado, olive oil, lemon juice, honey, basil, parsley, mint, and 1 tablespoon water. Blend on medium speed until smooth, about 20 seconds. Season with salt and pepper.

2. In a large bowl, combine the honeydew, watermelon, cantaloupe, cucumber, and onion. Drizzle the dressing over the salad and gently toss to coat evenly. Finish with the toasted pistachios, additional herbs, flaky salt, and pepper.

Make It a Spread! *Serve alongside the Crostini with Chèvre, Prosciutto, Nectarines, Honey, and Basil (page 30) and Early Riser Plate (page 145).*

Sweet Peach and Corn Salad

Peach season in upstate New York is my favorite time of year. From early July to late September, the farmers' markets are brimming with sweet, juicy peaches, ripe and ready to eat. One of the best ways to prepare peaches is to grill them. I'm not necessarily a grill master, so if I can do it, so can you. The natural sugars of the peaches caramelize to create a delicious char. When you combine them with Little Gem lettuce, you have the perfect amount of refreshing flavor and crunch. The honey Dijon vinaigrette really brings it all together, making this a bright and fresh summer staple.

SERVES 4 TO 6

- 2 ripe peaches, halved and pitted
- ⅓ cup plus 1 tablespoon extra-virgin olive oil
- 3 tablespoons balsamic vinegar
- 1 teaspoon Dijon mustard
- 1 teaspoon honey
- 1 garlic clove, minced
- Kosher salt and freshly ground black pepper
- 2 heads Little Gem lettuce, coarsely chopped
- 1 cup canned corn kernels, drained
- 1 cup fresh pearl mozzarella balls
- 1 small cucumber, thinly sliced
- 1 cup halved cherry tomatoes
- 2 tablespoons chopped fresh dill
- 2 tablespoons thinly sliced fresh basil leaves

1. Heat a grill pan over medium heat or heat an outdoor grill to medium.
2. Brush the peach halves lightly with 1 tablespoon of the olive oil. Grill cut side down just until grill marks appear, 3 to 5 minutes. Remove, let cool slightly, and slice into wedges.
3. In a small bowl, whisk together the balsamic vinegar, remaining ⅓ cup olive oil, Dijon mustard, honey, and garlic and season with salt and pepper. Whisk well until emulsified. Taste and adjust the seasoning as needed.
4. Place the Little Gem lettuce in a large serving bowl. Drizzle with most of the dressing and season with salt and pepper, tossing to coat. Add the corn, mozzarella, cucumber, and tomatoes. Arrange the grilled peach slices on top. Spoon over the remaining dressing and sprinkle with dill and basil. Gently toss everything to combine and serve.

Make It a Spread! *Serve alongside the Euro Summer Plate (page 153) and Summer Shrimp Cups (page 34).*

GRILLED STONE FRUIT AND HERBS

WINTER CITRUS AND TOASTED WALNUTS

PESTO, PROSCIUTTO, AND ROASTED RED PEPPERS

BURRATA BOWLS, THREE WAYS

EACH SERVES
4 TO 6

Some people might think burrata has been overdone—I respectfully disagree. Burrata is a staple in my fridge and appetizer creations. The best part? Cutting through the mozzarella exterior to reveal the stracciatella (cream and cheese curds) inside. I'll never forget the first time I served up burrata with pesto, prosciutto, and roasted red peppers at a party. My friends loved the pairing so much that it's now a highly requested app when I have gatherings. Whether it's paired with the summer sweetness of grilled stone fruit and fresh herbs, or a tangy burst of winter citrus, burrata offers a satisfying base to build upon. I always love to serve it with a baguette or toasted sourdough to soak up the silky goodness.

Burrata with Grilled Stone Fruit and Herbs

- 2 nectarines pitted and thinly sliced (see Note)
- 2 teaspoons honey
- 1 tablespoon extra-virgin olive oil, plus more for drizzling
- 2 (8-ounce) burrata balls
- 1 cup fresh cherries, pitted and halved
- ⅓ cup chopped fresh basil
- ⅓ cup chopped fresh mint
- Kosher salt and freshly ground black pepper
- French baguette, sliced, for serving

NOTE: Use whatever stone fruit is available and appealing! You can swap in two small peaches, four small apricots, or three small plums for the two nectarines.

1 Heat a grill pan over medium heat or heat an outdoor grill to medium.

2 In a small bowl, combine the nectarines and honey and stir to coat well. Brush the grill with the olive oil, then grill the apricots until charred on both sides and slightly softened, 2 to 3 minutes per side.

3 Place the burrata balls in a shallow serving dish. Arrange the grilled nectarines and cherries around the burrata. Drizzle olive oil over everything, top with basil and mint, and season with salt and pepper. Serve with baguette slices.

Make It a Spread! *Serve alongside the Sweet Peach and Corn Salad (page 102) and Chicken Sausage, Pepper, and Onion Bites (page 33).*

Burrata with Winter Citrus and Toasted Walnuts

- 2 (8-ounce) burrata balls
- 1 orange of your choice (such as navel, blood, or sumo), peeled and segmented into bite-size pieces
- ¼ cup pomegranate seeds
- 2 tablespoons extra-virgin olive oil
- 1 tablespoon honey
- 2 teaspoons fresh lemon juice
- ¼ cup walnuts, toasted and lightly crushed
- Chopped fresh mint, for serving
- Flaky salt
- Freshly ground black pepper
- French baguette, sliced, for serving

1 Place the burrata balls in a shallow bowl. Scatter the citrus and pomegranate seeds over the top.

2 In a small bowl, whisk together the olive oil, honey, and lemon juice.

3 Drizzle the dressing over the burrata and citrus. Scatter over the toasted walnuts and mint. Finish with flaky salt and pepper. Serve with baguette slices.

Make It a Spread! *Serve alongside the Smoked Mozzarella, Artichoke, and Pesto Focaccia Pizza (page 192) and Chopped Brussels and Pecorino Salad (page 125).*

Burrata with Pesto, Prosciutto, and Roasted Red Peppers

½ cup pesto

2 (8-ounce) burrata balls

¾ cup roasted red peppers, thinly sliced

4 slices prosciutto, torn in half lengthwise

¼ cup pine nuts, toasted

2 tablespoons balsamic glaze

Fresh basil leaves, for serving

French baguette, for serving

1 Spread the pesto over the bottom of a shallow serving bowl.

2 Place the burrata balls on top of the pesto. Scatter around the roasted red peppers, followed by the prosciutto, folded into flowers. Sprinkle the toasted pine nuts over everything. Drizzle with balsamic glaze, and top with fresh basil leaves. Serve with baguette slices.

Make It a Spread! *Serve alongside the Citrus and Crunchy Green Salad with Fennel and Pomegranate (page 126) and Salumi Pinwheel Platter (page 156).*

Creamy Peperoncini and Pickled Onion Potato Salad

In many Connecticut delis, long sandwiches are called "grinders." Also known as hoagies, subs, or simply sandwiches, one in particular stands out: the Italian grinder. The ingredients consist of a variety of salty salumi, provolone, and fresh lettuce, but the highlight is the dressing. Well, dressings. The grinder is always topped with mayo, olive oil, and red wine vinegar, and Italian seasoning—and I love to add a dash of spicy honey for flair. It's an addicting combination and goes well with many different recipes—including this potato salad. I love a bit of brine, so the peperoncini and pickled red onions add a zing to an otherwise simple potato salad.

SERVES 6

- 2 pounds baby potatoes
- Kosher salt
- ⅓ cup mayonnaise
- 1 tablespoon red wine vinegar
- 1 tablespoon extra-virgin olive oil
- ½ tablespoon spicy honey
- ¼ teaspoon dried oregano
- ¼ teaspoon dried basil
- ¼ teaspoon red pepper flakes
- Freshly ground black pepper
- ½ cup pickled thinly sliced red onions, homemade (see page 77) or store-bought
- ¼ cup sliced peperoncini
- 2 tablespoons chopped fresh dill
- 3 scallions, finely chopped

1. Place the potatoes in a large pot and cover with cold water. Add a pinch of salt. Bring to a boil over medium-high heat, then reduce the heat to low and simmer until fork-tender, 10 to 12 minutes. Drain the potatoes and let cool slightly.
2. Meanwhile, in a small bowl, whisk together the mayonnaise, vinegar, olive oil, spicy honey, oregano, basil, red pepper flakes, and a pinch each of salt and pepper. Taste and adjust the seasonings as needed.
3. Cut the cooked potatoes into bite-size pieces and transfer to a large serving bowl. Add the pickled red onions, peperoncini, dill, and scallions. Pour in the dressing and gently toss to coat. Season with more salt and pepper as needed. Cover the potato salad and refrigerate for at least 30 minutes before serving to allow the flavors to meld. Serve cold or at room temperature.

Make It a Spread! *Serve alongside the Chicken Sausage, Pepper, and Onion Bites (page 33) and Sweet Peach and Corn Salad (page 102).*

Tarragon Egg Salad

WITH SEEDED NUTTY CRUMBLE

I am a cold-deli-salad superfan. Homemade egg salads, tuna salads, chicken salads, pasta salads—you name it. Add a side of crackers and you've got yourself a great meal. There are many ways to make an egg salad, but my version has a creamy egg base with an herbaceous twist thanks to fresh tarragon—and instead of crackers alongside, it has a crunchy blend of nuts and seeds for texture. Serve with fresh veggies and get ready for this to be your new favorite variation.

SERVES 4

- 6 large eggs
- 3 tablespoons mayonnaise
- 1 teaspoon Dijon mustard
- 1 teaspoon grainy mustard
- 1 teaspoon fresh lemon juice
- Kosher salt and freshly ground black pepper
- 1 tablespoon finely chopped fresh tarragon, plus more for serving
- 1 small shallot, finely minced
- ¼ cup hulled sunflower seeds
- ¼ cup hulled pumpkin seeds
- 2 tablespoons white sesame seeds
- 2 tablespoons finely chopped walnuts
- 1 teaspoon extra-virgin olive oil
- ½ teaspoon flaky salt
- ½ teaspoon red pepper flakes
- Sliced cucumbers, for serving

Make It a Spread! *Serve alongside the Potato Pancakes with a Smoky Twist (page 23) and Cucumber Bites with Boursin, Smoked Salmon, Lemon Zest, and Dill (page 46).*

1. Fill a large bowl with ice and water and set it nearby. Place the eggs in a medium saucepan and cover with water. Bring to a boil over medium-high heat, then reduce the heat to low and cook for 8 minutes. Using a slotted spoon, transfer the eggs to the ice bath to cool for 5 minutes, then peel and coarsely chop the eggs.

2. In a large bowl, whisk together the mayonnaise, both mustards, lemon juice, and a pinch each of salt and pepper. Stir in the tarragon and shallot. Add the chopped eggs and gently fold to incorporate.

3. In a small skillet, combine the sunflower seeds, pumpkin seeds, sesame seeds, and walnuts. Drizzle with olive oil and sprinkle with flaky salt and red pepper flakes. Cook over medium heat, stirring frequently, until golden and fragrant, about 6 minutes. Transfer to a small bowl and let cool.

4. Spoon the egg salad into a shallow bowl and generously scatter with the seeded nutty crumble over the top. Sprinkle with more tarragon and serve with sliced cucumbers alongside.

My Favorite Chicken Salad

When I was growing up, my parents always had some sort of chicken salad in the fridge, and I loved to pile it high on a sandwich, scoop it up with crackers, or simply enjoy it straight from the bowl with a fork. This version, an old favorite of mine, is full of surprises. In one bite you might taste the sweet pop of a dried cranberry, a fresh morsel of celery, or the big crunch of pecans. Serve this at a tasty brunch party alongside crispy fruit-and-nut crackers to enhance what's inside.

SERVES 4 TO 6

- 1 tablespoon extra-virgin olive oil
- 2 (8-ounce) boneless, skinless chicken breasts
- Kosher salt and freshly ground black pepper
- ¼ cup mayonnaise
- 2 tablespoons plain full-fat Greek yogurt
- 1½ tablespoons honey mustard
- 1 teaspoon apple cider vinegar
- 1 celery stalk, finely diced
- ½ small red onion, finely diced
- ½ cup dried cranberries
- ¼ cup pecans, toasted and coarsely chopped
- Fruit-and-nut crackers, for serving (I like Raincoast Crisps)

1. In a medium skillet, heat the olive oil over medium heat. Season the chicken breasts all over with salt and pepper. When the oil is shimmering, add the chicken and cook until no longer pink and an instant-read thermometer inserted into the thickest part reads 165°F, 6 to 7 minutes per side. Transfer to a cutting board and let cool slightly.

2. Meanwhile, in a large bowl, whisk together the mayonnaise, yogurt, honey mustard, and apple cider vinegar. Season with salt and pepper.

3. Use tongs or two forks to shred the chicken and add it to the large bowl along with the celery, red onion, dried cranberries, and toasted pecans. Toss gently to combine and coat well with the dressing. Cover the chicken salad and refrigerate for at least 30 minutes before serving to allow the flavors to meld. Serve with crackers alongside.

Make It a Spread! *Serve alongside the Zesty Feta and Melon Skewers (page 45) and Spring Fling Plate (page 139).*

HERBY FETA AND
GRILLED CHICKEN
AUTUMNAL GOAT
CHEESE AND
SQUASH
MOZZARELLA
AND CHICKEN
SAUSAGE

PASTA SALAD, THREE WAYS

✸

EACH SERVES
4 TO 6

Pasta Salad Summer is a big deal in my house. As soon as the weather starts to warm up, bowlfuls of cold pasta hit the table. It's one of the more versatile and riffable dishes out there, with countless shapes and mix-ins to choose from. When considering pasta salad pairings, I always like to start with the cheese because, well, have you met me? The best pasta salad cheese is either fresh or extremely aged—nothing in between. Some fresh favorites include mozzarella, feta, and goat cheese, which have a smooth, satisfying texture and flavor that won't overpower. For aged, I love shredded Parmigiano-Reggiano or shredded Pecorino Romano. Next, some meat: I love something salty here, like crispy prosciutto or sautéed chicken sausage, which will contrast nicely against whatever fresh and/or pickled produce you choose to add. Fresh herbs are also a great addition, and no pasta salad is complete without the dressing. A creamy or zesty vinaigrette sets the base tone in every bite, and deepens the flavor as the dish marinates. The pasta salads will keep in the refrigerator in an airtight container for up to 3 days. Just be sure to toss with additional dressing before serving if the texture seems dry.

Mozzarella and Chicken Sausage Summer Pasta Salad

Kosher salt

8 ounces cavatappi pasta

3 chicken sausages, sliced into ⅓-inch-thick coins

6 to 8 asparagus spears, trimmed and cut on an angle into ½-inch-thick slices

½ cup plain full-fat Greek yogurt

¼ cup mayonnaise

1 tablespoon extra-virgin olive oil

1 garlic clove, minced

2 teaspoons fresh lemon juice

2 teaspoons white wine vinegar

Freshly ground black pepper

1 cup fresh pearl mozzarella balls

1 cup halved cherry tomatoes

½ cup frozen sweet corn, thawed

1 tablespoon chopped fresh parsley

1 tablespoon chopped fresh dill

½ tablespoon chopped fresh chives

1 Bring a large pot of salted water to a boil over high heat. Add the pasta and cook until al dente according to the package directions. Drain and rinse with cold water.

2 Meanwhile, in a medium pan, cook the chicken sausage in a single layer over medium heat until lightly browned, 6 to 8 minutes, flipping halfway through. Transfer to a plate.

3 Using the same pan, cook the asparagus, stirring occasionally, until bright green and tender, 5 to 6 minutes. Transfer to the plate with the chicken sausage.

4 In a small bowl, whisk together the yogurt, mayonnaise, olive oil, garlic, lemon juice, and white wine vinegar. Season with salt and pepper.

5 Place the cooked pasta in a large serving bowl. Drizzle with a bit of the dressing and toss to coat. Add the chicken sausage, asparagus, mozzarella, cherry tomatoes, and corn. Pour in the remaining dressing and gently toss to combine and coat well. Refrigerate for up to 30 minutes before serving for the flavors to meld. Stir in the parsley, dill, and chives right before serving.

Make It a Spread! *Serve alongside the Sweet Peach and Corn Salad (page 102) and Tajín-Watermelon and Halloumi Skewers (page 43).*

Herby Feta and Grilled Chicken Pasta Salad

Kosher salt

8 ounces mezzi rigatoni pasta

4 tablespoons extra-virgin olive oil

2 (8-ounce) boneless, skinless chicken breasts

Freshly ground black pepper

2 tablespoons fresh lemon juice

1 tablespoon spicy honey

1 tablespoon Dijon mustard

1 garlic clove, minced

¼ teaspoon red pepper flakes

5 ounces feta cheese, crumbled

1 cup marinated artichoke hearts, chopped

2 Persian cucumbers, diced

1 cup halved cherry tomatoes

½ cup pickled red onions, homemade (see page 77) or store-bought

2 tablespoons chopped fresh dill

2 tablespoons chopped fresh parsley

1. Bring a large pot of salted water to a boil over high heat. Add the pasta and cook until al dente according to the package directions. Drain and rinse with cold water.

2. In a medium pan, heat 1 tablespoon of the olive oil over medium heat. Season the chicken breasts all over with salt and pepper. When the oil is shimmering, add the chicken and cook until an instant-read thermometer inserted into the thickest part reads 165°F, 6 to 7 minutes per side. Transfer to a cutting board and let cool slightly, then cut into cubes.

3. Meanwhile, in a small bowl, whisk together the remaining 3 tablespoons olive oil, the lemon juice, spicy honey, Dijon, garlic, and red pepper flakes and season with salt and pepper.

4. Place the cooked pasta in a large serving bowl. Drizzle with a bit of the dressing and toss to coat. Add the chicken, feta, artichokes, cucumbers, tomatoes, and pickled onions. Pour in the remaining dressing and gently toss to combine and coat well. Refrigerate for up to 30 minutes before serving for the flavors to meld. Stir in the dill and parsley right before serving.

Make It a Spread! *Serve alongside the Crostini with Chèvre, Prosciutto, Nectarines, Honey, and Basil (page 30) and Melon Ball Summer Salad (page 101).*

Autumnal Goat Cheese and Squash Pasta Salad

1½ cups diced (1-inch) peeled butternut squash (half of a small)

¼ cup plus 1 tablespoon extra-virgin olive oil

3 tablespoons maple syrup

Kosher salt and freshly ground black pepper

8 ounces orecchiette pasta

3 slices prosciutto

1 tablespoon fresh lemon juice

3 ounces goat cheese, crumbled

½ large carrot, thinly sliced into ribbons with a vegetable peeler

¼ cup pecans, toasted

1 cup arugula

1 Preheat the oven to 400°F. Line a baking sheet with parchment paper or aluminum foil.

2 In a medium bowl, toss the squash with 1 tablespoon of the olive oil, 1 tablespoon of the maple syrup, and a pinch each of salt and pepper. Spread on the prepared baking sheet in a single layer and roast for about 10 minutes. Carefully use tongs or a spatula to flip the pieces, and continue cooking for 5 to 10 minutes more, until the squash is lightly browned and easily pierced with a fork.

3 Bring a large pot of salted water to a boil over high heat. Add the pasta and cook until al dente according to the package directions. Drain and rinse with cold water.

4 In a medium pan, cook the prosciutto over medium-high heat until crispy, about 3 minutes per side. Remove from the heat and let cool, then crumble with your hands.

5 In a small bowl, whisk together the remaining ¼ cup olive oil, the remaining 2 tablespoons maple syrup, and the lemon juice and season with salt and pepper.

6 Place the cooked pasta in a large serving bowl. Drizzle with a bit of the dressing and toss to coat. Add the goat cheese, prosciutto crumbles, squash, carrot ribbons, and pecans. Pour in the remaining dressing and gently toss to combine and coat well. Refrigerate for up to 30 minutes before serving for the flavors to meld. Toss in the arugula right before serving.

Make It a Spread! *Serve alongside the Root Vegetable Soup Coupes (page 129) and Veggie Meatballs with Pesto (page 57).*

Autumn Harvest Cobb Salad

This salad is wonderful for your fall gatherings, cozy dinner parties, or Friendsgiving feasts. While a traditional cobb features bacon, chicken, hard-boiled eggs, avocado, tomatoes, and blue cheese, this recipe has an autumnal twist: butternut squash, sweet dried cranberries, and crunchy walnuts. Instead of topping with bacon, we mix it into the sweet and zesty maple vinaigrette—it's my favorite part of this recipe.

SERVES 4 TO 6

- 4 bacon slices
- 1½ cups diced (1-inch) peeled butternut squash (half of a small)
- ½ cup plus 1 tablespoon extra-virgin olive oil
- Kosher salt and freshly ground black pepper
- ⅓ cup maple syrup
- 3 tablespoons apple cider vinegar
- 2 teaspoons honey mustard
- 2 heads romaine lettuce, chopped
- 2 cups shredded chicken breast
- 3 large hard-boiled eggs, quartered
- 1 cup diced Persian cucumber (about 3)
- ½ cup dried cranberries
- 2 ounces blue cheese, crumbled
- ⅓ cup walnuts, toasted and chopped

1. Preheat the oven to 400°F. Line two baking sheets with parchment paper or aluminum foil.
2. Arrange the bacon slices in an even layer on the first prepared baking sheet. On the second prepared baking sheet, toss the squash with 1 tablespoon of the olive oil and a pinch each of salt and pepper. Arrange in an even layer.
3. Roast the bacon and squash together for 20 to 25 minutes, carefully using tongs or a spatula to flip everything halfway through, until the bacon is crispy and the squash is lightly browned and pierces easily with a fork. Let cool slightly, then finely crumble the bacon.
4. In a small bowl, whisk together the remaining ½ cup olive oil, the maple syrup, apple cider vinegar, and honey mustard until smooth and emulsified. Add the crumbled bacon and season with salt and pepper.
5. Place the romaine in a large serving bowl. Drizzle with a bit of the dressing and toss to coat. Season with a pinch each of salt and pepper. Top the romaine with separate piles of chicken, hard-boiled eggs, squash, cucumber, dried cranberries, blue cheese, and toasted walnuts. Just before serving, pour in the remaining dressing and gently toss to combine and coat well.

Make It a Spread! *Serve alongside the Root Vegetable Soup Coupes (page 129) and Sweet Potato and Turkey Casserole (page 94).*

Chopped Brussels and Pecorino Salad

Typically during the holidays, there's an overload of cheesy, meaty dishes. This salad is a welcome contrast, providing a fresh crunch with bright flavor. Finely chopped Brussels sprouts and kale provide a solid foundation, softening under a zesty honey-lemon dressing. Aged Pecorino Romano brings its signature salty and sharp crystalline notes, creating a lovely pairing against the sweet and tart cranberries. Toasted almonds add another layer of crunch, nodding to the subtle nuttiness of the cheese. The result is a dish that's both festive and nourishing.

SERVES 4 TO 6

---

2 tablespoons extra-virgin olive oil, plus more for massaging

2 tablespoons honey

2 tablespoons fresh lemon juice

1 tablespoon Dijon mustard

Kosher salt and freshly ground black pepper

1 bunch kale, leaves stemmed and roughly torn

8 ounces Brussels sprouts, shredded

½ cup freshly grated Pecorino Romano cheese

¼ cup almonds, toasted and chopped

½ cup dried cranberries

1. In a small bowl, whisk together the olive oil, honey, lemon juice, Dijon, and a pinch each of salt and pepper until smooth and well combined.

2. Place the kale leaves in a large bowl, drizzle with olive oil, and massage for about 1 minute to soften them. Add the Brussels sprouts. Drizzle with a bit of the dressing and toss to coat. Season with a pinch each of salt and pepper. Add the cheese, toasted almonds, and dried cranberries. Pour in the remaining dressing and gently toss to combine and coat well. Serve immediately or refrigerate for 15 to 20 minutes to allow the flavors to meld.

Make It a Spread! *Serve alongside the Smoked Mozzarella, Artichoke, and Pesto Focaccia Pizza (page 192) and Veggie Meatballs with Pesto (page 57).*

Citrus and Crunchy Green Salad

WITH FENNEL AND POMEGRANATE

It took me an embarrassingly long amount of time to learn that citrus season was in the wintertime. Oranges reach peak ripeness between November and March, making for a bright and tangy addition to your cold-weather snack spreads. Crisp butter lettuce and fennel are accompanied by toasted slivered almonds, with sweet, tart citrus and pomegranate seeds. Obviously, we still need a little cheese in here, so the goat cheese dressing ties it all together.

SERVES 4 TO 6

---

2 ounces fresh goat cheese, at room temperature

⅓ cup extra-virgin olive oil

2 tablespoons red wine vinegar

1 tablespoon fresh lemon juice

1 tablespoon honey

1 teaspoon dried thyme

Kosher salt and freshly ground black pepper

4 cups torn butter lettuce leaves (bite-size pieces)

1 small fennel bulb, cored and thinly sliced, fronds reserved for serving

1 blood orange, halved and thinly sliced

¼ cup pomegranate seeds

¼ cup slivered almonds, toasted

1. In a small bowl, whisk together the goat cheese, ⅓ cup of the olive oil, the vinegar, lemon juice, honey, and thyme until smooth and creamy. Season with salt and pepper.
2. Place the lettuce in a large serving bowl, drizzle with a bit of the dressing, and toss to coat. Season with a pinch each of salt and pepper. Add the sliced fennel, blood orange, and pomegranate seeds. Pour in the remaining dressing and gently toss to combine and coat well. Top with the toasted almonds and fennel fronds and serve immediately.

Make It a Spread! *Serve alongside the Winter Holiday Antipasto (page 175) and Ricotta, Prosciutto, Fig Jam, and Arugula Focaccia Pizza (page 193).*

Root Vegetable Soup Coupes

Serving soup is an unexpected party trick—and instead of using up all my bowls, I like to ladle the soup into small coupe glasses for guests to sip on as they mingle. I call them soup coupes—no utensils required! My dad has been making this root vegetable soup for years, and it's my favorite soup when I'm craving something cozy and rich. The sautéed root vegetables and onions create a sweet and savory base, and the dollop of cream and crispy sage elevate the finish.

SERVES 6 TO 8

---

4 tablespoons (½ stick) unsalted butter

1 small rutabaga, peeled and chopped

1 medium Gala apple, peeled and chopped

1 small yellow onion, coarsely chopped

1½ cups diced (1-inch) peeled butternut squash (half of a small)

2 medium carrots, chopped

1 small sweet potato, peeled and chopped

Kosher salt and freshly ground black pepper

2 cups low-sodium chicken stock

½ cup heavy cream, plus more for serving

2 tablespoons maple syrup

Cayenne pepper

1 tablespoon extra-virgin olive oil

8 to 12 fresh sage leaves

1. In a large Dutch oven, melt the butter over medium-high heat. Add the rutabaga, apple, onion, squash, carrots, and sweet potato. Season with salt and pepper. Cook, stirring occasionally, until the onions are soft and translucent, 7 to 8 minutes. Add the stock and bring to a boil, then reduce the heat to maintain a simmer and cook until all the vegetables are cooked through and tender, 20 to 25 minutes.

2. Use an immersion blender to puree the vegetables directly in the pot until smooth. (Alternatively, carefully transfer to a high-speed blender, blend, and return to the pot.) Add the cream and maple syrup and season with salt, black pepper, and cayenne pepper. Return the soup to a simmer to warm through.

3. Meanwhile, heat the olive oil in a small pan over medium-high heat until shimmering. Add the sage leaves in an even layer. Cook until crispy and beginning to brown, 10 to 15 seconds per side. Transfer to a paper towel–lined plate to drain and immediately sprinkle with salt.

4. Ladle the soup into coupe glasses, dividing evenly. Finish with an extra drizzle of cream, the crispy sage leaves, and some black pepper.

Make It a Spread! *Serve alongside the Chopped Brussels and Pecorino Salad (page 125) and Red Wine Poached Pears (page 64).*

Ricotta and Spinach Savory Pudding

Don't sleep on savory pudding—it's a delightful and unexpected dish to serve as a fun brunch appetizer. This one is almost a cheesy quiche hybrid, full of creamy notes. Grana Padano is one of my favorite hard Italian cheeses. It looks like a Parmigiano-Reggiano, but the flavor is milder with a slightly sweeter taste. It blends wonderfully with the ricotta here, while the lemon and dill add balance. Toasted pine nuts lend the finishing touch with a buttery and earthy crunch.

SERVES 4 TO 6

- Nonstick cooking spray
- 2 cups loosely packed fresh baby spinach
- 1½ cups whole-milk ricotta cheese
- 3 large eggs
- ½ cup plain full-fat Greek yogurt
- 1 tablespoon fresh lemon juice
- ¼ cup freshly shredded Grana Padano cheese
- ½ teaspoon garlic powder
- Kosher salt and freshly ground black pepper

FOR SERVING

- ¼ cup pine nuts, toasted
- Zest of 1 lemon
- Flaky salt
- Fresh dill

1 Preheat the oven to 375°F. Coat an 8-inch square baking dish with cooking spray.

2 In a large skillet, cook the spinach over medium heat, stirring, until the leaves have wilted and any excess moisture has evaporated from the pan, 3 to 4 minutes. Remove from the heat and let cool slightly.

3 In a large bowl, whisk together the ricotta, eggs, yogurt, lemon juice, Grana Padano, garlic powder, and a pinch each of salt and pepper until smooth and well combined. Stir in the spinach until evenly incorporated. Pour the ricotta mixture into the prepared baking dish. Smooth out the top with a spatula.

4 Bake the pudding for 45 minutes, until set and slightly golden around the edges. Remove from the oven and let cool slightly. Top with the toasted pine nuts, lemon zest, flaky salt, and dill. Serve warm, scooped into bowls.

Make It a Spread! *Serve alongside the Potato Pancakes with a Smoky Twist (page 23) and Early Riser Plate (page 145).*

BOARDS

THE HUMBLE BOARD is where I got my start while building my company That Cheese Plate, serving up elaborate designs with my signature rustic crumbles, salami rivers, and produce ponds. Here you'll find some of my favorite classic themed boards, using That Cheese Plate's signature Cheese by Numbers method, as well as other creative ways to plate up pizza, sandwiches, galettes, and more. Boards bring a sense of shared joy to the table, inviting guests to gather and savor each bite together. Whether you're going for something elegant or rustic, no two boards ever look the same. Make them about experimenting and letting your personality come through in the details. Treat your board like a canvas with the food as the paint—it will double as a detailed centerpiece to complete your tablescape.

Truffle Cheddar Breakfast Quesadillas

Besides happy hour, breakfast might be my favorite meal of the day. This breakfast quesadilla combines what I love most about morning meals. Crispy slices of bacon are layered with scrambled eggs and truffle cheddar, making for a warm, salty, and smoky base. The pickled red onions, homemade jalapeño avocado salsa, and cilantro contrast with tang and acidity. It's a great dish to make in batches and serve while guests mingle at brunchtime.

SERVES
4 TO 6

- 8 bacon slices
- 6 large eggs
- Kosher salt and freshly ground black pepper
- 3 tablespoons unsalted butter
- 1 ripe avocado
- 1 jalapeño, seeded and coarsely chopped
- 2 tablespoons full-fat sour cream
- Juice of ½ small lime
- 1 garlic clove
- ¼ cup fresh cilantro, plus more for serving
- 4 large flour tortillas
- 6 ounces truffle cheddar, shredded (see Note)
- 1 cup pickled red onions, homemade (see page 77) or store-bought, plus more for serving

1. Preheat the oven to 400°F. Line a baking sheet with parchment paper or aluminum foil.
2. Arrange the bacon on the prepared baking sheet in an even layer and bake for 15 minutes, until crispy. Transfer to a paper towel–lined plate to drain and cool.
3. Meanwhile, crack the eggs into a medium bowl, season with salt and pepper, and whisk. In a large skillet, melt 1 tablespoon of the butter over medium heat. Pour in the eggs and cook, stirring frequently to scramble, until just set, about 1 minute. Transfer the eggs to a bowl.
4. In a food processor, combine the avocado, 2 tablespoons water, jalapeño, sour cream, lime juice, garlic, and cilantro. Process until smooth, 30 seconds. Season with salt and pepper.

Recipe continues

NOTE: If you can't find truffle cheddar, this recipe works great with sharp cheddar, pepper Jack, or smoked cheddar!

5 In the same skillet you used to cook the eggs (no need to wipe it out), melt ½ tablespoon butter over medium heat. Working with one at a time, lay a tortilla flat in the skillet. On one half of the tortilla, layer on a quarter each of the scrambled eggs, bacon, cheddar, and pickled red onions. Fold over the tortilla to cover and cook until golden brown on the outside and the cheese is melted inside, 1 to 2 minutes per side. Remove the quesadilla from the pan and slice into three triangles, arranging them on a board. Repeat with the remaining ingredients, adding the remaining butter to the skillet between each quesadilla.

6 Sprinkle the quesadillas with cilantro, then top with pickled red onions and a hefty drizzle of the creamy jalapeño salsa. Serve the remaining salsa alongside for dipping.

Make It a Spread! *Serve alongside the Cucumber Bites with Boursin, Smoked Salmon, Lemon Zest, and Dill (page 46) and Charcuterie Cream Cheese (page 89).*

THE CHEESE BY NUMBERS METHOD

Each board in this chapter is styled using my foolproof six-step method.

1. Cheese
2. Meat
3. Produce
4. Crunch
5. Dip
6. Garnish

The steps are associated with numbers on the ingredient list and photos to make board building easy, with an impressive result!

Spring Fling Plate

SERVES 4

This plate heralds the peak days of spring. My house has a decent-size backyard, and in the dead of winter when the trees are bare, I can see pretty much every detail of my neighbors' yards. When spring arrives, everything changes. The leaves form light green buds and flowers emerge from their slumber. This transformation really makes the dark days of winter worth it. To celebrate the best time of year, we have two fresh cheeses paired with spring produce. Prosciutto adds subtly sweet charcuterie, with flatbread crackers for crunch. Garnish with a variety of fresh herbs and edible flowers to make the plate pop.

1: CHEESE

6 ounces feta cheese

1 (5-ounce) package Garlic & Fine Herbs Boursin cheese

2: MEAT

5 slices prosciutto

3: PRODUCE

1 large nectarine, sliced

2 Persian cucumbers, sliced into coins

10 small strawberries

4: CRUNCH

7 flatbread crackers, plus more for serving

5: DIP

3 ounces honey

6: GARNISH

Fresh mint

Edible violas

Make It a Spread! *Serve alongside the Spring Pea and Arugula Potato Salad (page 97) and Garlic Lover's Dip (page 80).*

1

4

2

3

5

6

Goat Cheese Galette

WITH PROSCIUTTO AND SPRING VEGGIES

If you're looking to host a classy soiree with low effort, a galette is a must-have in the appetizer spread. Originating in France, galettes are rustic and approachable, making them a favorite for both making and eating. This version features tangy goat cheese and lemon, paired with salty prosciutto, marinated artichokes, and fresh asparagus. The flavors remind me of early spring days, when the sun begins to set later in the day. It's a dish with buttery notes that make the fresh produce pop.

SERVES 4 TO 6

- 1 (8.5-ounce) sheet frozen puff pastry, thawed
- 4 ounces goat cheese, at room temperature
- Zest of 1 lemon
- 1 tablespoon chopped fresh dill, plus more for serving
- 4 slices prosciutto
- ½ cup chopped marinated artichoke hearts
- 4 asparagus spears, trimmed and cut into 2-inch pieces
- ½ small yellow onion, thinly sliced
- 1 tablespoon extra-virgin olive oil, plus more for serving
- Kosher salt and freshly ground black pepper
- 1 large egg, beaten

Make It a Spread! *Serve alongside Cucumber Bites with Boursin, Smoked Salmon, Lemon Zest, and Dill (page 46) and Melon Ball Summer Salad (page 101).*

1. Preheat the oven to 400°F. Line a baking sheet with parchment paper.
2. Roll out the puff pastry into a 12-inch square on the prepared baking sheet.
3. Place the goat cheese in a small bowl, add the lemon zest and dill, and stir to combine. Crumble the goat cheese mixture evenly over the center of the puff pastry, leaving a ½-inch border all the way around. Lay the prosciutto slices on top of the goat cheese mixture, then scatter over the artichokes, asparagus, and onion. Drizzle all over with the olive oil and season with salt and pepper.
4. Carefully fold the edges of the pastry over the filling. Brush the pastry with the beaten egg.
5. Bake the galette for 35 to 40 minutes, until the pastry is golden brown and crispy. Remove from the oven and let cool slightly before slicing. Sprinkle with fresh dill and drizzle with olive oil, then serve.

Early Riser Plate

SERVES 4

This plate feels like a morning stroll through the farmers' market, with ingredients that I like to mark the start of the day. Nutty Gruyère and a bright tarragon egg salad are at the heart of this spread, accompanied by crisp cucumbers, juicy cherry tomatoes, and sliced French radishes. Sourdough bread brings it all together, ready to be slathered with whipped salted butter or sweet strawberry jam. Seeded crackers add a satisfying crunch, while fresh herbs and edible flowers provide a final, elegant flourish. It's a little bit of breakfast, a little bit of lunch, and a whole lot of flavor.

1: CHEESE

6 ounces Gruyère cheese, sliced into triangles

2: PROTEIN

Tarragon Egg Salad with Seeded Nutty Crumble (page 112) or store-bought egg salad

3: PRODUCE

2 Persian cucumbers, sliced

8 multicolored cherry tomatoes, halved or whole

4 French radishes, sliced lengthwise

4: CRUNCH

½ medium loaf fresh sourdough bread, sliced

Seeded crackers

5: DIP

3 ounces strawberry jam

3 ounces salted whipped butter

6: GARNISH

Fresh tarragon leaves

Edible flowers (I like violas and flowering herbs)

Make It a Spread! *Serve alongside the Potato Pancakes with a Smoky Twist (page 23) and Cucumber Bites with Boursin, Smoked Salmon, Lemon Zest, and Dill (page 46).*

2

3

5

6

Snacks for Dinner Plate

SERVES 2 TO 4

Potato chips and pickles for dinner? Yes please. This plate is all about casual, crave-able bites that are great for sharing when you don't feel like cooking a robust meal. Snack plates aren't just an easy way to graze—they're also a stress-free way to dine in. Unwrap from the fridge, maybe slice a few items, and enjoy. Havarti and mini mozzarella balls meet savory deli turkey rolls for a protein-packed base. The zippy mix of pickles and peperoncini adds a crunchy contrast, while wavy potato chips and baguette slices bring just the right comfort-food vibes. A side of honey mustard is the dipping companion, and a touch of fresh basil makes it all feel just a little bit elevated.

1: CHEESE

6 ounces Havarti cheese, thinly sliced

6 ounces marinated mini mozzarella balls

2: MEAT

6 slices deli turkey, folded

3: PRODUCE

6 half-sour pickles: 4 kept whole, 2 sliced lengthwise

10 bread-and-butter pickle chips

6 peperoncini

4: CRUNCH

2 cups wavy potato chips, plus more for serving

1 small baguette, sliced, some on the board with more on the side

5: DIP

3 ounces honey mustard

6: GARNISH

Fresh basil leaves

Make It a Spread! *Serve alongside the Elevated Potato Chips (page 49) and Buffalo Chicken Meatballs (page 38).*

2

3

5

6

Euro Summer Plate

SERVES 4 TO 6

I was fortunate to spend a few summers in Europe, and whether it's aperitivo in Italy, aperó in France, or tapas in Spain, each culture celebrates the act of slowing down, reflecting on the day, and enjoying good company over good food. On this plate, marinated feta and nutty Manchego set the tone, paired with a savory mortadella. Sweet red cherries, honeydew melon, and green grapes contrast the briny pop of Castelvetrano olives. Taralli crackers and sliced baguette offer a satisfying crunch, while a drizzle of balsamic glaze layers in some sweetness. Garnished with fresh basil, this spread is as elegant as it is effortless, ideally accompanied by a glass of crisp white wine.

1: CHEESE

6 ounces Manchego cheese, sliced into triangles

6 ounces marinated goat or feta cheese

2: MEAT

8 slices mortadella

3: PRODUCE

10 red cherries

½ small honeydew melon, seeded and scooped into balls

16 Castelvetrano olives

2 small bunches green grapes

4: CRUNCH

½ cup taralli crackers, plus more for serving

1 medium French baguette, sliced

5: DIP

3 ounces balsamic glaze

6: GARNISH

Fresh basil leaves

Edible flowers (I used daisies)

Make It a Spread! *Serve alongside the Summer Shrimp Cups (page 34) and Tuna Tartare Bites (page 37).*

NOTE: Serve with a small ramekin on the side to collect the cherry and olive pits.

2

3

5

6

Salumi Pinwheel Platter

These salumi pinwheels are a fun take on a classic Italian sandwich, which encompasses some of my favorite flavor pairings. If I spotted a platter of these at a party, you'd find me parked right beside them. Salty and savory salumi is cut with a smooth provolone, while the giardiniera dressing captures the essence of briny roasted red peppers and gherkins. The mayo adds a creamy element, contrasted by the fresh crunchy lettuce. These are the best bites to serve at a luncheon or gathering where you're looking for a bit more substance.

MAKES
24 PINWHEELS

---

4 (12-inch) flour tortillas

24 thin slices Italian dry salami

16 slices mortadella

12 slices prosciutto

8 slices provolone cheese

4 large romaine leaves

2 tablespoons giardiniera

½ cup mayonnaise

1 tablespoon Dijon mustard

1 teaspoon red wine vinegar

¼ teaspoon garlic powder

¼ teaspoon onion powder

¼ teaspoon dried oregano

Kosher salt and freshly ground black pepper

Make It a Spread! *Serve alongside the Burrata with Pesto, Prosciutto, and Roasted Red Peppers (page 108) and Veggie Meatballs with Pesto (page 57).*

1. On a clean work surface, lay out 1 tortilla. Evenly layer on 6 slices of salami, 4 slices of mortadella, 3 slices of prosciutto, and 2 slices of provolone. Overlap the slices slightly to ensure full, even coverage, leaving a ¼-inch border all around the edges.

2. Lay the romaine leaf lengthwise over the provolone, with the stem end pointing in the same direction you'll roll the tortilla (rolling with the grain of the lettuce helps it stay intact and makes for a smoother wrap). Carefully roll the tortilla tightly into a log, holding the filling in place as you go. Repeat steps 1 and 2 with the remaining tortillas, meat, cheese, and romaine.

3. Once rolled, use a sharp knife to trim the uneven ends of each log to create clean, uniform slices. Cut each rolled tortilla into 1-inch slices to form the pinwheels. If desired, insert a toothpick into each pinwheel to ensure they stay intact. Arrange on a board.

4. In a food processor, combine the giardiniera, mayonnaise, Dijon mustard, and vinegar. Pulse until smooth. Stir in the garlic powder, onion powder, and oregano and season with salt and pepper. Transfer the dip to a small bowl and serve alongside the pinwheels for dipping or drizzling.

NOTE: These pinwheels can be prepared up to 6 hours in advance and stored in the refrigerator. Wrap the logs tightly in plastic wrap before slicing to keep them fresh and help them hold their shape

Simple Shop Plate

SERVES 4 TO 6

Have you ever found yourself wandering the grocery store aisles, overwhelmed and unsure where to begin your cheese plate? This one is your answer to stress-free hosting. With a sharp aged cheddar and creamy Brie as the base, it comes together with just a handful of simple ingredients. Hard salami provides a savory and salty depth, while sweet dried apricots and juicy blueberries add fruity balance. Seeded crackers act as the textural crunch while the fig jam ties it all together. Finish it off with simple herbs from the produce aisle, and this board is proof that simplicity can be stunning!

1: CHEESE

6 ounces aged cheddar cheese, roughly cubed

1 (8-ounce) wheel Brie cheese, half sliced into triangles

2: MEAT

8 ounces hard salami, thinly sliced

3: PRODUCE

14 dried apricots, some halved

½ cup fresh blueberries

4: CRUNCH

Seeded crackers

⅓ cup salted roasted almonds

5: DIP

3 ounces fig jam

6: GARNISH

Fresh thyme sprigs

Fresh rosemary sprigs

Make It a Spread! *Serve alongside the Citrus and Crunchy Green Salad with Fennel and Pomegranate (page 126) and Caprese with Salami Skewers (page 42).*

2

3

5

6

Happiest Hour Plate

SERVES 4 TO 6

I thrive during happy hour. As someone who prefers to be in bed on the earlier side, happy hour is the perfect time to wind down and connect with friends. This plate brings together a range of flavors to kick off your predinner parties. The rich, caramelized Gouda pairs beautifully with the salty soppressata, while the sharpness of Parmigiano-Reggiano offers a satisfying contrast to the sweetness of the dried figs. Citrus-marinated olives bring a touch of brightness, while the pretzel chips and corn nuts add a crunchy texture. Sweet and tangy orange marmalade and fresh thyme and micro marigolds round out this colorful plate. You might just get carried away and skip dinner all together!

1: CHEESE

6 ounces goat Gouda cheese, sliced into rectangles

6 ounces Parmigiano-Reggiano cheese, roughly cubed

2: MEAT

12 slices spicy soppressata

3: PRODUCE

¾ cup citrus-marinated olives, homemade (recipe follows) or store-bought

½ cup halved dried figs

4: CRUNCH

Pretzel chips

Toasted corn kernels, such as Corn Nuts

5: DIP

4 ounces orange marmalade

6: GARNISH

Fresh thyme sprigs

Fresh micro marigolds

Make It a Spread! *Serve alongside the White Bean Dip with Tapenade (page 82) and Citrus and Crunchy Green Salad with Fennel and Pomegranate (page 126).*

2

3

5

6

CITRUS-MARINATED OLIVES

MAKES 1 CUP

1 tablespoon extra-virgin olive oil

1 tablespoon thinly sliced orange zest

1 garlic clove, minced

4 thyme sprigs

¾ cup pitted Castelvetrano olives, partially crushed

2 tablespoons fresh orange juice

Kosher salt and freshly ground black pepper

Red pepper flakes

In a medium skillet, heat the olive oil over medium heat until shimmering. Add the orange zest, garlic, and thyme and cook, stirring, until fragrant, about 1 minute. Add the olives and cook until fragrant, 2 minutes more. Pour in the orange juice and season with salt, pepper, and red pepper flakes and simmer until most of the liquid evaporates, 2 to 3 minutes. Serve warm or refrigerate for 30 minutes in an airtight container.

Cozy Night In Plate

SERVES 4 TO 6

This cheese plate is made for those nights with friends where sweatpants are encouraged. We're not going to the bar; we're staying in and loving it. At the center is a warm, gooey wheel of baked Camembert, essential for dipping or spreading. Camembert has a slightly earthier flavor than Brie, its richness complemented by subtle mushroomy notes. Thinly sliced Italian salami brings a savory richness, while roasted garlic broccoli and crispy tater tots act as the savory cheese dippers. Tangy cornichons and grainy mustard cut through the richness, while slices of crusty baguette scoop up every bite.

1: CHEESE

1 (8-ounce) wheel Baked Camembert (recipe follows)

2: MEAT

1 (8-ounce) Italian dry salami, thinly sliced

3: PRODUCE

1½ cups frozen tater tots

1½ cups Roasted Garlic Broccoli (recipe follows)

½ cup cornichons with pearl onions

4: CRUNCH

1 medium French baguette, sliced

5: DIP

3 ounces grainy mustard

6: GARNISH

Fresh rosemary sprigs

Make It a Spread! *Serve alongside the Veggie Meatballs with Pesto (page 57) and Chopped Brussels and Pecorino Salad (page 125).*

2

3

5

6

COZY NIGHT IN PLATE PREP

1½ cups trimmed broccoli florets

1 tablespoon extra-virgin olive oil

1 teaspoon garlic powder

Kosher salt and freshly ground black pepper

1½ cups frozen tater tots

1 (8-ounce) wheel Camembert cheese

1 Position a rack in the top third of the oven and another in the center and preheat the oven to 400°F.

2 On a baking sheet, toss the broccoli florets with the olive oil and garlic powder and season with salt and pepper. Arrange in an even layer on one half of the baking sheet; add the tater tots to the other. Slice off the top rind of the Camembert and place in a small baking dish.

3 Bake the vegetables together on the center rack for about 15 minutes. Place the Camembert on the top rack and bake everything for about 10 minutes, until the vegetables are browned and crispy and the cheese is soft and bubbling.

4 Transfer the baking dish with the cheese to a heatproof platter and scatter the salami, tater tots, broccoli, cornichons, and baguette all around. Place the mustard in a small ramekin and add it to the board. Garnish with rosemary sprigs.

Winter Holiday Antipasto

SERVES 6 TO 8

Every year when the holidays roll around, I'm put on cheese plate duty . . . obviously. While I've made plenty of wreath- and tree-shaped boards over the years, nothing beats a simple antipasto spread loaded with Italian cheeses and marinated veggies. This one combines the sharpness of Pecorino Romano with smooth, fresh mozzarella. Marinated mushrooms and artichokes take you straight to an Italian deli, and the quick-pickled carrots add a nice, crunchy bite. Spicy soppressata, pepperoni, and olive tapenade bring in a little salty richness. It's a timeless classic.

1: CHEESE

6 ounces Pecorino Romano cheese, roughly cubed

6 ounces marinated ciliegine mozzarella balls

2: MEAT

16 thin slices spicy soppressata

10 thin slices pepperoni

3: PRODUCE

½ cup marinated mushrooms

¼ cup roasted red peppers

10 marinated artichoke hearts

10 pimiento-stuffed olives

¼ cup pickled carrots, homemade (see page 77) or store-bought

4: CRUNCH

1 baguette, torn into pieces

5: DIP

Olive tapenade, homemade (see page 82) or store-bought

6: GARNISH

Fresh thyme leaves

Fresh rosemary sprigs

Make It a Spread! *Serve alongside the Ricotta, Prosciutto, Fig Jam, and Arugula Focaccia Pizza (page 193) and Citrus and Crunchy Green Salad with Fennel and Pomegranate (page 126).*

2

3

5

6

Savory S'mores

Move over, marshmallows—it's time to roast some cheese over the open flame. One of my favorite parts of my backyard is the firepit. When I lived in New York City, I never had the ability to make a fire, let alone have access to any outdoor space, so now that I have both, I tend to spend many evenings in front of the flames. This platter is ideal for those who have a savory tooth. Forget the typical sweet and sticky campfire treats—this version celebrates the melted magic of smoked mozzarella, Brie, and young Gouda.

SERVES 6 TO 8

- 1 (6-ounce) wheel Brie cheese, sliced into 6 wedges, or 6 mini Brie wheels
- 6 ounces smoked mozzarella cheese, sliced into 1-inch-thick rectangles
- 6 ounces young Gouda cheese, sliced into 1-inch-thick rectangles
- 16 slices Italian dry salami
- 1 large apple, thinly sliced
- 1 medium French baguette, sliced
- 16 graham crackers
- 4 ounces fig jam
- 4 ounces spicy honey

PAIRINGS TO TRY

- Brie, apple, and fig jam on a graham cracker (creamy, crunchy, sweet, and spiced)
- Smoked mozzarella, salami, and spicy honey on a baguette slice (smoky, savory, spicy, and sweet)
- Gouda, apple, and spicy honey on a graham cracker (rich, tart, sweet, and spiced)

1. Place the cheeses, salami, apple, baguette, and graham crackers on a large board.
2. Fill two 3-ounce ramekins, one with fig jam and one with spicy honey, and add to the board.
3. Use a long wooden stick or metal skewer to roast the cheese over an open flame. Keep an eye on the cheese—it will melt quickly!
4. Assemble your preferred bite and enjoy immediately while warm.

Make It a Spread! *Serve alongside the Pumpkin Pie Dip (page 90) and Maple-Candied Bacon Deviled Eggs (page 61).*

LEMON CURD, RASPBERRIES, AND SHORTBREAD CRUMBLE
FIG JAM, CRISPY PROSCIUTTO, AND SLIVERED ALMONDS
HONEY MUSTARD, PISTACHIOS, AND THYME

BAKED BRIE, THREE WAYS

✶

EACH SERVES 6 TO 8

Baked Brie is my love language. When baked, it takes on a velvety, luscious texture. It's my go-to appetizer for cozy nights in or impromptu gatherings with friends. What I love most is how Brie's flavor pairs with so many toppings. For something sweet and savory, you can't go wrong with the classic combination of fig jam and prosciutto. For a nostalgic twist, I love to bake Brie with honey mustard and toasted pistachios, a recipe my mom used to make for family parties. If I'm in the mood for something unexpected, I'll top baked Brie with tangy lemon curd, fresh raspberries, and crumbled shortbread cookies for a dessert-like treat. The possibilities really are endless, which is probably why I'll never get tired of it.

Baked Brie with Fig Jam, Crispy Prosciutto, and Slivered Almonds

1 (8-ounce) wheel Brie cheese

2 tablespoons fig jam

¼ cup slivered almonds

6 slices prosciutto

Chopped fresh rosemary, for serving

Baguette slices, for serving

1 Preheat the oven to 350°F.

2 Place the Brie in a small oven-safe dish. Score the top by slicing a grid pattern with the tip of a knife. Cover the top of the Brie with the fig jam and slivered almonds. Bake the Brie for 12 to 15 minutes, until the center is soft and gooey but the cheese is still holding its shape.

3 Meanwhile, arrange the prosciutto on a baking sheet in an even layer. Bake for 15 minutes, until crispy. Remove and let cool slightly.

4 Crumble the prosciutto over the Brie. Sprinkle with rosemary and serve immediately with baguette slices alongside.

NOTE: If you really want to elevate your Brie baking experience, try wrapping Brie in a sheet of puff pastry and bake for 30 to 35 minutes for a golden, flaky masterpiece.

Make It a Spread! *Serve alongside the Citrus and Crunchy Green Salad with Fennel and Pomegranate (page 126) and Veggie Meatballs with Pesto (page 57).*

Baked Brie with Lemon Curd, Raspberries, and Shortbread Crumble

1 (8-ounce) wheel Brie cheese

2 tablespoons lemon curd

½ cup raspberries

3 shortbread cookies, crushed (I like Walker's)

½ tablespoon thinly sliced fresh mint leaves

Water crackers, for serving

1. Preheat the oven to 350°F.
2. Place the Brie in a small oven-safe dish. Score the top by slicing a grid pattern with the tip of a knife. Cover the top of the Brie with the lemon curd.
3. Bake the Brie for 12 to 15 minutes, until the center is soft and gooey but the cheese is still holding its shape.
4. Arrange the raspberries over the lemon curd, gently pressing them into the surface. Sprinkle the crushed shortbread cookies and fresh mint leaves on top. Serve immediately with water crackers alongside.

Make It a Spread! *Serve alongside the Crostini with Chèvre, Prosciutto, Nectarines, Honey, and Basil (page 30) and Red Wine Poached Pears (page 64).*

Baked Brie with Honey Mustard, Pistachios, and Thyme

1 (8-ounce) wheel Brie cheese

2 tablespoons honey mustard

¼ cup crushed shelled pistachios

Fresh thyme leaves, for serving

Baguette slices, for serving

1 Preheat the oven to 350°F.

2 Place the Brie in a small oven-safe dish. Score the top by slicing a grid pattern with the tip of a knife. Cover the top of the Brie with the honey mustard and crushed pistachios.

3 Bake the Brie for 12 to 15 minutes, until the center is soft and gooey but the cheese is still holding its shape.

4 Sprinkle with thyme and serve immediately with baguette slices alongside.

Make It a Spread! *Serve alongside the Chopped Brussels and Pecorino Salad (page 125) and Buffalo Chicken Meatballs (page 38).*

Fresh and Zesty Veggies

A veggie platter is a reliable and vibrant appetizer to balance other savory dishes. I love to take advantage of the farmers' markets upstate for my fresh produce. Supporting local makers and shopping seasonally is always an adventure. Depending on the time of year, the veggies rotate, but they always taste like nature's candy. A little olive oil, salt, and lemon juice go a long way, adding brightness to the veggies while leaving their pure flavor intact. You'll most likely never make the same exact plate twice, which makes local crudités that much more special.

SERVES 4 TO 6

---

3 Persian cucumbers, sliced

8 red radishes, thinly sliced (you can also use watermelon radishes or purple radishes)

1 cup sugar snap peas, trimmed

1 cup yellow cherry tomatoes

4 rainbow carrots, sliced

Leaves of 2 small endives

2 tablespoons extra-virgin olive oil

Zest and juice of ½ large lemon

Flaky salt

Freshly ground black pepper

FOR SERVING

Fresh dill sprigs

Fresh parsley sprigs

Viola or chamomile flowers

Dips of your choice

1 Arrange the cucumbers, radishes, sugar snap peas, cherry tomatoes, carrots, and endives on a board. Drizzle with the olive oil and lemon juice, sprinkle on the lemon zest, and finish with a touch of flaky salt and some pepper.

2 Garnish with fresh herbs and edible flowers and serve with dips of your choice.

Make It a Spread! *Serve alongside the Garlic Lover's Dip (page 80) and Creamy Eggplant Dip (page 81).*

RICOTTA, PROSCIUTTO, FIG JAM, AND ARUGULA
SMOKED MOZZARELLA, ARTICHOKE, AND PESTO

FOCACCIA PIZZA, THREE WAYS

EACH SERVES 4 TO 6

Pizza is the perfect communal meal, offering a wide variety of toppings to suit every palate. Instead of a bar crawl, my friends and I go on "pizza crawls" in New York City, which are always a hit. As for parties, pizza is extremely easy to share and serve, making it a great handheld without the fuss of forks and knives. What makes this pizza special is the focaccia dough. Focaccia is softer and fluffier than regular pizza dough, due to its longer proofing (or rising) time. This gives it a pillowy texture while still maintaining a crispy crunch out of the oven. Pizza topping combinations are endless and can be a debate for many, but I narrowed down my favorites into three distinctly flavored pizzas.

Sausage, Pepper, and Onion Focaccia Pizza

- 1 tablespoon extra-virgin olive oil
- 2 sweet Italian sausages, casings removed
- 1 small yellow onion, thinly sliced
- ½ red bell pepper, thinly sliced
- ½ green bell pepper, thinly sliced
- Kosher salt and freshly ground black pepper
- 1 (13 × 18-inch) focaccia, homemade (recipe follows) or store-bought
- 1 cup tomato sauce
- 1½ cups shredded part-skim mozzarella cheese
- ½ cup freshly grated pecorino cheese
- ⅓ cup sliced black olives
- 1 teaspoon dried oregano
- Spicy honey, for serving

1 Preheat the oven to 450°F.

2 In a large skillet, heat the olive oil over medium heat. Add the sausage and cook, breaking it up with a wooden spoon, until browned and cooked through, 8 to 10 minutes. Transfer to a medium bowl. In the same skillet (no need to wipe it out), cook the onion and peppers over medium-high heat, stirring occasionally, until softened and slightly caramelized, 8 to 10 minutes. Season with salt and black pepper and transfer to the bowl with the sausage.

3 Place the focaccia on a rimmed baking sheet and spread the tomato sauce evenly over the top. Sprinkle on the mozzarella and pecorino cheese. Add the caramelized onions and peppers, crumbled sausage, and olives. Sprinkle with the oregano. Bake for 10 to 15 minutes, until the cheese is bubbling and the edges of the focaccia are golden brown.

4 Drizzle the spicy honey over the pizza before serving.

Make It a Spread! *Serve alongside the Chopped Brussels and Pecorino Salad (page 125) and Stuffed Mushroom Dip (page 69).*

FOCACCIA

MAKES ONE FOCACCIA, ABOUT 13 × 18 INCHES

3½ cups all-purpose flour

1 teaspoon kosher salt

2 teaspoons sugar

1 (¼-ounce) packet instant yeast

1¼ cups warm water

2 tablespoons extra-virgin olive oil, plus more for greasing and drizzling

1 In a large bowl, combine the flour, salt, sugar, and yeast. Add the warm water and olive oil, then mix with a whisk or fork until a shaggy dough forms.

2 Turn the dough out onto a floured surface and continue to fold and press the dough with your hand until smooth, about 6 minutes. Grease a large bowl with olive oil. Place the dough in the bowl, cover with a damp towel, and let rise at room temperature until doubled in size, 1 to 1½ hours.

3 Generously grease a standard 13 × 18-inch rimmed baking sheet with olive oil.

4 Turn the dough out onto the prepared pan and gently press it into an even layer, covering the entire pan. Drizzle additional olive oil over the top of the dough and let it rest for an additional 30 minutes to rise slightly.

5 Meanwhile, preheat the oven to 450°F.

6 After the second proof, spread so the dough fills the pan, drizzle with more olive oil, and dimple all over with your fingertips.

7 Bake the focaccia for 12 to 15 minutes, until the top is just beginning to set but is not fully browned. Proceed to your toppings of choice!

Smoked Mozzarella, Artichoke, and Pesto Focaccia Pizza

- 1 (13 × 18-inch) focaccia, homemade (page 191) or store-bought
- 1 (7-ounce) jar pesto
- 6 ounces smoked mozzarella cheese, shredded
- ¾ cup chopped marinated artichoke hearts
- 3 ounces Parmigiano-Reggiano cheese, shredded
- 1 teaspoon dried oregano
- Balsamic glaze, for serving
- Fresh basil, for serving

1. Preheat the oven to 450°F.
2. Place the focaccia on a rimmed baking sheet and spread the pesto evenly over the top. Sprinkle on the smoked mozzarella, artichoke hearts, Parmigiano-Reggiano, and oregano.
3. Bake for 10 to 15 minutes, until the cheese is bubbling and the edges of the focaccia are golden brown.
4. Just before serving, top the pizza with balsamic glaze and fresh basil.

Make It a Spread! *Serve alongside the Garlic Lover's Dip (page 80) and Fresh and Zesty Veggies (page 187).*

Ricotta, Prosciutto, Fig Jam, and Arugula Focaccia Pizza

- 1 cup whole-milk ricotta cheese
- ½ cup shredded part-skim mozzarella cheese, plus more for topping
- 1 teaspoon garlic powder
- 1 teaspoon dried oregano
- Zest of 1 lemon
- Kosher salt and freshly ground black pepper
- 1 cup arugula
- 2 teaspoons fresh lemon juice
- 1 tablespoon extra-virgin olive oil
- 1 (13 × 18-inch) focaccia, homemade (page 191) or store-bought
- 3 ounces fig jam
- 6 slices prosciutto, torn in half lengthwise

1. Preheat the oven to 450°F.
2. In a small bowl, combine the ricotta, mozzarella, garlic powder, oregano, and lemon zest and season with salt and pepper. Stir until smooth.
3. In a separate small bowl, toss the arugula with the lemon juice and olive oil and season with salt and pepper.
4. Place the focaccia on a rimmed baking sheet and spread the ricotta mixture evenly over the top. Add swirls of fig jam over the cheese. Top with torn prosciutto slices and more mozzarella. Bake for 10 to 15 minutes, until the prosciutto begins to crisp.
5. Top with the dressed arugula and serve.

Make It a Spread! *Serve alongside the Spring Pea and Arugula Potato Salad (page 97) and Handheld Pasta Salad (page 50).*

Maple Tofu and Squash Sandwiches

This plant-based sandwich will make you love and appreciate tofu even more than before. Pressing tofu before cooking releases its moisture, allowing it to develop a better crust when seared. Add the maple sriracha glaze, and tofu transforms into a delightful base (the glaze also makes for a great wing sauce). For the quintessential fall sandwich, delicata squash makes an appearance accompanied by a balsamic mayo, lemony arugula, and red onion to top.

MAKES 4 SANDWICHES

- 1 (16-ounce) block extra-firm tofu
- Kosher salt and freshly ground black pepper
- 1 small delicata squash, seeded and sliced into ½-inch half rings
- 3½ tablespoons extra-virgin olive oil
- 2 tablespoons maple syrup
- 2 tablespoons low-sodium soy sauce
- 1 tablespoon sriracha
- 2 garlic cloves, minced
- ¼ cup mayonnaise
- 1 tablespoon balsamic glaze
- 2 cups loosely packed arugula
- 1 small red onion, thinly sliced
- 1 tablespoon fresh lemon juice
- 1 large ciabatta loaf, halved lengthwise

1 Preheat the oven to 400°F.

2 Press the tofu by wrapping it in paper towels, placing it on a plate, and weighing it down with a heavy object like a cast-iron skillet. Let it sit for at least 30 minutes, changing the paper towels as needed. Once pressed, slice the tofu crosswise into ½-inch-thick pieces and season with salt and pepper.

3 Meanwhile, on a baking sheet, toss the squash with 1 tablespoon of the olive oil and season with salt and pepper. Arrange in an even layer. Roast the squash for 20 to 25 minutes, using tongs or a spatula to flip halfway through, until tender and golden brown.

4 In a small bowl, whisk together the maple syrup, soy sauce, sriracha, garlic, and ½ tablespoon olive oil and season with salt and pepper. In a separate small bowl, whisk together the mayonnaise and balsamic glaze until smooth. Season with salt and pepper.

Recipe continues

Make It a Spread! *Serve alongside the Autumn Harvest Cobb Salad (page 122) and Garlic Lover's Dip (page 80).*

5 In a medium skillet, heat 1 tablespoon olive oil over medium heat until shimmering. Add the tofu and cook, turning occasionally, until all sides are golden and crispy, 3 to 4 minutes per side. Pour in the maple glaze and cook until the glaze thickens, 1 to 2 minutes.

6 In a medium bowl, combine the arugula and onion. Toss with the remaining 1 tablespoon olive oil and the lemon juice and season with salt and pepper.

7 Spread a generous amount of balsamic mayo on both sides of the ciabatta. Layer one side with the tofu, squash, and arugula salad, reserving 2 squash rings. Drizzle with any leftover glaze from the pan. Close the sandwich and cut evenly into 4 sandwiches.

8 Secure each sandwich with a long toothpick. Cut the reserved squash rings in half and add a piece on top of each sandwich.

Roast Beef Sliders

WITH EMMENTAL, PICKLES, AND HORSERADISH CREMA

These little sandwiches are versatile enough to serve at your game-day celebrations, or for a warm holiday feast. They're a fan favorite in my house and make for a delicious centerpiece while served on a platter. The key: Use high-quality cheese and slice it by hand. It takes a little bit more effort but is totally worth it. The horseradish crema adds quite the kick, while the savory roast beef and pickles balance out the intensity. Generously drizzle with a Dijon butter sauce and bake to perfection.

MAKES 12 SLIDERS

- 1 cup full-fat sour cream
- 2 tablespoons prepared horseradish
- 2 teaspoons Tabasco sauce
- 2 teaspoons fresh lemon juice
- Kosher salt and freshly ground black pepper
- 12 slider buns
- 1 pound deli roast beef
- 6 slices Emmental cheese, halved
- 24 bread-and-butter pickle chips
- 2 tablespoons salted butter, melted
- 1 teaspoon Dijon mustard
- 1 teaspoon poppy seeds

1. Preheat the oven to 350°F.
2. In a small bowl, whisk together the sour cream, horseradish, Tabasco, and lemon juice and season with salt and pepper to make the crema.
3. Slice the slider buns in half. Place the bottom halves in a large baking dish. Spread a thin layer of the horseradish crema across the buns. Layer each with a slice of roast beef, Emmental cheese, and two pickle chips. Spread horseradish crema on the inside of the top buns and close the sandwiches. In a small bowl, stir together the melted butter and Dijon mustard. Brush the tops of the slider buns with the butter mixture and sprinkle with the poppy seeds.
4. Cover the sliders loosely with aluminum foil and bake for 10 minutes. Remove the foil and bake for 5 to 7 minutes more, until the cheese is melted and the tops of the sliders are golden.
5. Remove from the oven and let cool slightly. Serve warm with extra horseradish crema alongside for dipping.

Make It a Spread! *Serve alongside the Caramelized Onion Dip with Herbs (page 93) and Pineapple Cowboy Caviar (page 85).*

The Best Tuna Sandwiches

I love tuna salad and I'm proud of it. Anyone who actively goes out of their way to hate on canned tuna needs to find a new hobby. I've been trying to master my tuna recipe for years, and I finally achieved greatness with this one. To me, a harmonious tuna sandwich has a balance of creaminess, brine, zest, and tang. The tuna salad itself has a wide variety of mix-ins, from peperoncini to shredded carrot and basil. Butter lettuce and slightly sweet pickles create a fresh crunch between the soft sourdough, with salt-and-vinegar chips to serve, naturally. Don't forget to garnish your sandwiches! I like a skewer of peperoncini on top.

MAKES 4 SANDWICHES

- 3 (5-ounce) cans tuna, drained
- ⅓ cup mayonnaise
- 2 tablespoons grainy mustard
- 11 peperoncini: 3 thinly sliced, 8 kept whole for serving
- ½ medium carrot, shredded
- 8 fresh basil leaves
- 1 tablespoon balsamic glaze
- 1 teaspoon garlic powder
- Kosher salt and freshly ground black pepper
- 8 slices sourdough bread
- 12 butter lettuce leaves
- 1 cup bread-and-butter pickle chips
- 1 cup pickled thinly sliced red onions, homemade (see page 77) or store-bought
- 1 (7-ounce) bag salt-and-vinegar potato chips, for serving

NOTE: If you want a little extra crunch, add the chips directly onto the sandwich!

1 In a food processor, combine the tuna, mayonnaise, and grainy mustard. Pulse until well combined but some texture remains. Add the sliced peperoncini, shredded carrot, basil, balsamic glaze, and garlic powder and season with salt and pepper. Pulse to mix evenly.

2 On a slice of fresh sourdough, add a generous heap of tuna, followed by 3 butter lettuce leaves, ¼ cup of the pickle chips, and ¼ cup of the pickled onions. Close the sandwich with the other slice of bread. Slice in half and secure each sandwich half with a long toothpick skewered with peperoncini. Repeat with the other three sandwiches.

3 Arrange the sandwiches on a platter and serve with salt-and-vinegar potato chips.

Make It a Spread! *Serve alongside the Creamy Peperoncini and Pickled Onion Potato Salad (page 111) and Elevated Potato Chips (page 49).*

BEVERAGES

ALONG WITH WELCOMING GUESTS with an appetizer, I always greet them with a drink. A welcome drink sets the tone, letting your guests know they can relax and enjoy the party. I like to prepare beverages for my guests—it's a small gesture that makes a big impact, whether as simple as pouring a glass of wine or as involved as shaking up a cold martini.

Dirty Vodka Martini

WITH CHEESE SKEWERS, THREE WAYS

I love martinis. I can't explain the magic that happens when you mix ice-cold vodka and olive juice, but it does things to me . . . and I'm not the only one. I've seen my fair share of wildly dirty martinis over the years, some even resembling salad dressing, but I prefer paring back the drink a bit and leaving the big burst of flavors to the garnishes. Think of this as an appetizer in a cocktail. Take a little sip of the martini, and maybe a little bite of salami with Gruyère: best of both worlds. I like to rest my skewer on top of the martini, but if you're feeling wild you can plop it in to soak up some of the salty vodka.

MAKES
1 COCKTAIL

Ice cubes

Dry vermouth, for rinsing

3 ounces vodka

1 ounce olive juice, plus more to taste

Place ice in a martini glass, then place in the freezer to chill. Meanwhile, in an ice-filled cocktail shaker, add a splash of dry vermouth. Shake for about 5 seconds, then strain. (The vermouth rinse is mainly just to coat the ice.) Add the vodka and olive juice to the shaker and shake vigorously until ice cold, 20 seconds. Strain into the chilled martini glass and garnish with your choice of combinations on a toothpick:

- 1 cube Gruyère cheese + 1 pimiento-stuffed olive + 1 folded salami slice
- 1 cube sharp cheddar cheese + 1 cornichon + 1 folded prosciutto slice
- 1 blue cheese–stuffed olive + 1 slice roasted red pepper + 1 marinated mushroom

Try Pairing with . . . *Potato Pancakes with a Smoky Twist (page 23), Elevated Potato Chips (page 49), or Cheesy Puff Pastry Pinwheels (page 53).*

THE TCP

(TEQUILA, CLUB, PINEAPPLE)

When I don't feel like drinking a martini (it's rare, but it happens), a tequila, club soda, and pineapple juice is my next request. I enjoy margaritas on a case-by-case basis, but this combination is never too citrusy, never too sweet, and always hits the spot. For this recipe, I've added a bit of a twist. Muddled roasted pineapple and mezcal infuse each sip with a stunning smokiness, while the club soda, pineapple, and lime cut through the intensity. If you're not a fan of mezcal, tequila blanco works well, too.

MAKES
2 COCKTAILS

- 1½ cups cubed fresh pineapple
- ½ teaspoon extra-virgin olive oil
- Ice cubes
- 4 ounces mezcal
- 4 ounces fresh pineapple juice
- 1 ounce fresh lime juice
- 4 ounces club soda
- 2 lime wedges, for garnish
- 2 pineapple leaves, for garnish (optional)

1. Preheat the oven to 400°F. Line a baking sheet with aluminum foil.
2. Arrange the pineapple on the prepared baking sheet and drizzle with olive oil. Roast for 15 minutes, flipping halfway through, until golden and caramelized. Remove from the oven and let cool for 10 minutes.
3. Transfer the roasted pineapple to a cocktail shaker and muddle until broken down. Add the ice, mezcal, pineapple juice, and lime juice. Shake vigorously to chill, 15 seconds, then strain into two ice-filled glasses, dividing evenly.
4. Top each glass with club soda and garnish with a lime wedge and a pineapple leaf, if you'd like.

N/A Swap: *Omit the mezcal; add ginger beer.*

Try Pairing with . . . *Pineapple Cowboy Caviar (page 85), Melon Ball Summer Salad (page 101), or Happiest Hour Plate (page 163).*

Gin and Blackberry Tonic

This is my take on the classic gin and tonic with a fruity, herbaceous twist! Gin has beautiful notes of juniper and other botanicals, which complement the natural sweetness of the blackberries, enhanced by a dash of homemade basil simple syrup.

MAKES
1 COCKTAIL

- 5 fresh blackberries
- ½ ounce Basil Simple Syrup (recipe follows)
- 3 fresh basil leaves
- Ice cubes
- 2 ounces gin
- 1 ounce fresh lime juice
- 2 ounces tonic water
- 1 basil sprig, for garnish

In a cocktail shaker, combine the blackberries, simple syrup, and basil leaves and muddle until well combined. Add ice, followed by the gin and lime juice. Shake vigorously to chill, 15 seconds, then strain into a coupe glass. Top with the tonic water. Garnish with the basil sprig.

N/A Swap: *Omit the gin; add additional tonic water.*

Try Pairing with . . . *Zesty Feta and Melon Skewers (page 45), Burrata with Grilled Stone Fruit and Herbs (page 106), or Herby Feta and Grilled Chicken Pasta Salad (page 119).*

BASIL SIMPLE SYRUP

MAKES 4 OUNCES

- ½ cup sugar
- ½ cup fresh basil leaves

In a small saucepan, combine the sugar, basil, and ½ cup water. Bring to a boil over medium heat and cook, stirring constantly, until the sugar has completely dissolved. Reduce the heat to low and simmer until fragrant and slightly thickened, about 3 minutes. Remove from the heat and let steep for 30 minutes. Pour the syrup through a fine-mesh strainer into a glass jar, discarding the solids. Let cool in the refrigerator for at least 1 hour before using. Seal and store in the fridge for up to 4 weeks.

Select Spritz

You can catch me drinking a Select spritz all summer long. I'm not the biggest Aperol fan—it tends to be too sweet for my liking. Select, on the other hand, is the perfect middle ground. It's not as bitter as Campari and is elevated by the subtle sweetness of the Prosecco. I also just love the look of a bright red spritz with an orange slice and a green olive. It transports me right to a café in Italy!

MAKES 1 COCKTAIL

- Ice cubes
- 3 ounces Select Aperitivo (you can also use Campari or Aperol)
- 2 ounces Prosecco
- 1 ounce soda water
- Orange slice and green olive, for garnish (optional)

Fill a large wine glass with ice. Add the Select, followed by the Prosecco, then the soda water. Stir gently to combine. Garnish with an orange slice and a green olive, if you'd like.

Try Pairing with . . . *the Euro Summer Plate (page 153), Burrata with Pesto, Prosciutto, and Roasted Red Peppers (page 108), or Summer Shrimp Cups (page 34).*

Grapefruit and Rosemary Fizz

This light and fizzy drink is a great year-round cocktail to enjoy alongside a variety of different appetizers. The bright grapefruit is fruity and fresh for the summertime, while the rosemary infuses woodsy notes of herbs for the colder winter months. If you're not a vodka fan, this also tastes great with gin or tequila.

MAKES 1 COCKTAIL

- 2 sprigs rosemary
- 2 slices grapefruit, cut into quarters
- Ice cubes
- 2 ounces fresh grapefruit juice
- 1½ ounces vodka
- 1 teaspoon honey
- Club soda, for topping

In a cocktail shaker, combine the leaves of one of the rosemary sprigs and all but one of the grapefruit quarters. Gently muddle to release the juices and oils. Fill the shaker with ice and pour in the grapefruit juice, vodka, and honey. Shake vigorously to chill, 15 seconds, then strain into a tall, ice-filled glass. Top with club soda and garnish with the remaining rosemary sprig and reserved grapefruit wedge.

N/A Swap: *Omit the vodka; add ½ ounce fresh lime juice.*

Try Pairing with . . . *Burrata with Winter Citrus and Toasted Walnuts (page 107), The Best Tuna Sandwiches (page 200), or Stuffed Mushroom Dip (page 69).*

Minty Peach Green Tea Lemonade

This drink is my take on an Arnold Palmer, ideal for sipping on a sunny afternoon. Ripe summer peaches and lemonade are balanced out by strong green tea, brightened with mint and a hint of lime. The tea has earthy and grassy notes, grounding the sweetness of the drink. Sip and enjoy over ice for a nice refresh.

MAKES 2 DRINKS

- 1 green tea bag
- 1 ripe peach, peeled, halved, and pitted
- Sugar
- 6 fresh mint leaves, plus more for garnish
- ½ ounce fresh lime juice
- Ice cubes
- 4 ounces lemonade
- Lemon slices, for garnish

1 Bring 6 ounces water to a boil in a small kettle over high heat. Place the tea bag in a large mug or other heatproof vessel and pour over the boiling water. Let steep for 3 to 5 minutes. Discard the bag and let the tea cool in the refrigerator for 10 to 15 minutes.

2 Meanwhile, in a high-speed blender, combine the peach halves with a pinch of sugar and blend on high speed until smooth, 25 seconds. Add a drizzle of water to thin it out as needed.

3 In a cocktail shaker, muddle the mint leaves with the lime juice. Fill the shaker with ice, then add the cooled green tea, peach puree, and lemonade. Shake vigorously until chilled, 15 seconds, then strain into two tall, ice-filled glasses. Garnish with mint leaves and lemon slices. Add sugar to taste.

Try Pairing with . . . *Sweet Peach and Corn Salad (page 102), Burrata with Grilled Stone Fruit and Herbs (page 106), or Tarragon Egg Salad with Seeded Nutty Crumble (page 112).*

Dark Chocolate Tequila Espresso Martini

When I order an espresso martini, I know the night is going somewhere—and when it's an espresso martini made with tequila, all bets are off. This martini is a favorite for when the snacky party is winding down, and the group is heading to the next location. It's also a great drink to start off the night with something sweet. I also have nothing against a little espresso martini at brunch . . . after all, it's basically an iced coffee!

MAKES 1 COCKTAIL

- Ice cubes
- 1½ ounces reposado tequila
- 1 ounce espresso or cold brew
- 1 ounce coffee liqueur
- ½ ounce dark chocolate liqueur
- Dark chocolate, for serving
- 3 espresso beans, for serving

Place ice in a martini glass, then place in the freezer to chill. Meanwhile, fill a cocktail shaker with ice. Add the tequila, espresso, coffee liqueur, and dark chocolate liqueur. Shake vigorously until well chilled and frothy, 15 to 20 seconds. Strain into the chilled martini glass. Grate dark chocolate over the top and float 3 espresso beans on the surface.

Try Pairing with . . . *Savory S'mores (page 178), Baked Brie with Lemon Curd, Raspberries, and Shortbread Crumble (page 183), or Pumpkin Pie Dip (page 90).*

Spiced Pomegranate Bourbon Sour

This is the ideal drink to sip by a fire. The spiced notes of cinnamon and nutmeg are met with frothy egg white, while the tart pomegranate and lemon juices are mellowed by the caramelized notes of bourbon. A sweet Luxardo cherry on top completes the moment.

MAKES 2 COCKTAILS

- 4 ounces bourbon or rye whiskey
- 2 ounces pomegranate juice
- 1 ounce fresh lemon juice
- 1 ounce honey
- ¼ teaspoon ground cinnamon
- ¼ teaspoon ground nutmeg
- 1 large egg white
- Ice cubes
- 4 Luxardo cherries, for garnish

In a cocktail shaker, combine the bourbon, pomegranate juice, lemon juice, honey, cinnamon, nutmeg, and egg white. Shake vigorously without ice until the egg white is emulsified and frothy, 10 to 15 seconds. Add ice to the shaker and shake again until chilled, 15 to 20 seconds more. Strain into ice-filled rocks glasses or straight-up in coupe glasses. Garnish with the cherries.

Try Pairing with . . . *Red Wine Poached Pears (page 64), Winter Holiday Antipasto (page 175), or Sausage, Pepper, and Onion Focaccia Pizza (page 190).*

of the Sea

Classic Punch Bowl

Ah, the punch bowl—the timeless classic, and my favorite communal beverage. Here, we're channeling the retro charm of 1950s parties where the punch bowl was the centerpiece at every gathering. This recipe features light and dark rum paired with orange and pineapple juices, with club soda to add a little fizz. Cucumber, strawberry, and lemon can be found frozen inside the ice (party trick!), ready to melt and dance into the drink alongside the blood oranges and mint sprigs. Time to party!

SERVES 6 TO 8

½ small lemon, thinly sliced and cut into quarters

1 Persian cucumber, thinly sliced

6 strawberries, hulled and quartered

1 cup filtered water (or enough to fill an ice tray or muffin tin)

1 cup light rum

1 cup dark rum

2 cups fresh orange juice

2 cups fresh pineapple juice

Juice of 4 limes

2 cups club soda

Blood orange slices and mint springs, for serving

1 In a large square cube ice tray or muffin tin, evenly divide the lemon, cucumber, and strawberries. Pour over enough filtered water to fill. Place in the freezer until fully set, at least 3 hours.

2 In a large glass bowl, combine both rums, the orange juice, pineapple juice, and lime juice. Stir to mix well. Carefully pop the ice cubes out of their tray into the punch bowl. Just before serving, pour in the club soda and stir gently to combine.

3 Float blood orange slices and mint sprigs over the punch. Ladle into individual glasses to serve.

Try Pairing with . . . *Maple-Candied Bacon Deviled Eggs (page 61), Herby Feta and Grilled Chicken Pasta Salad (page 119), or the Euro Summer Plate (page 153).*

Snacky Party Menus

Below are a variety of curated recipe combinations to build a well-balanced seasonal spread. For each menu, I used my APPS method (see page 16) to ensure your bases are covered. From springtime garden parties to welcoming the first warm day of the year to cozy pizza parties in the depths of winter, there's a menu for every mood.

SPRING

The Brunch Club

- **AMBIENCE:** Set the tone with soft morning or midday light. Add tea lights or taper candles for a cozy touch. Opt for acoustic or soothing instrumental music, reminiscent of a coffee shop.
- **PRESENTATION:** Use soft linen napkins, pastel-colored platters, and tiered trays to evoke a tea party. Scatter small bud vases with wildflowers for pops of color.
- **PAIRINGS:** Highlight fresh, tangy, savory, creamy, and zesty dishes.
- **SPACE:** Create an inviting indoor space near sunny windows, accented with soft cushions.

BITES

Potato Pancakes with a Smoky Twist *23*

Crostini with Ricotta, Smoked Salmon, Green Peas, Lemon, and Dill *28*

Cucumber Bites with Boursin, Smoked Salmon, Lemon Zest, and Dill *46*

BOWLS

Charcuterie Cream Cheese *89*

Tarragon Egg Salad with Seeded Nutty Crumble *112*

Ricotta and Spinach Savory Pudding *130*

BOARDS

Truffle Cheddar Breakfast Quesadillas *135*

Goat Cheese Galette with Prosciutto and Spring Veggies *143*

Early Riser Plate *145*

BEVERAGES

Grapefruit and Rosemary Fizz *213*

Minty Peach Green Tea Lemonade *214*

Classic Punch Bowl *221*

The Garden Party

- **AMBIENCE:** Embrace the natural light of spring afternoons with candles and tea lights. Play calming acoustic music or singer-songwriter tunes.
- **PRESENTATION:** Use tiered trays, floral platters, and a white lace tablecloth accented with tulip-filled bud vases.
- **PAIRINGS:** Highlight fresh, vibrant, herbaceous flavors with tart and zesty dishes.
- **SPACE:** Host outdoors in the garden if warm, or in a sunlit room for early spring gatherings.

BITES

BOWLS

BOARDS

BEVERAGES

SUMMER

Alfresco Hour

- **AMBIENCE:** Host during the golden hour to enjoy the soft glow of the setting sun. Add fairy lights or string bulbs overhead, and place tea lights in glass holders to create a warm atmosphere. For the playlist, upbeat indie rock or French pop sets the mood.
- **PRESENTATION:** Use rustic serving boards, colorful ceramic bowls, and a natural linen tablecloth. Incorporate seasonal greenery, like eucalyptus or olive branches, and place whole fruits like lemon and limes on the table.
- **PAIRINGS:** Highlight briny, zesty, herbaceous, salty, and savory dishes.
- **SPACE:** Arrange seating outdoors on a patio or in the garden. If it's chilly, have blankets or a small firepit nearby to keep guests comfortable as the evening cools.

BITES

Summer Shrimp Cups *34*

Tuna Tartare Bites *37*

Caprese with Salami Skewers *42*

BOWLS

Sweet Peach and Corn Salad *102*

Burrata with Grilled Stone Fruit and Herbs *106*

Creamy Peperoncini and Pickled Onion Potato Salad *111*

BOARDS

Euro Summer Plate *153*

Happiest Hour Plate *163*

Fresh and Zesty Veggies *187*

BEVERAGES

Dirty Vodka Martini with Cheese Skewers, Three Ways *205*

Gin and Blackberry Tonic *209*

Select Spritz *210*

Poolside Day Party

- **AMBIENCE:** Bright, sun-filled day. Use paper lanterns or string lights around the pool to turn on as the golden hour approaches. Pool parties call for the nostalgic throwback tunes. Throw on those early 2000's jams and late 90's pop rock.
- **PRESENTATION:** Use vibrant, colorful platters and bowls that pop against the blue poolside backdrop. Add bright, seasonal floral bouquets and a rustic, textured tablecloth.
- **PAIRINGS:** Highlight refreshing, zesty, bright, grilled, and bold dishes.
- **SPACE:** Use lounge chairs and comfy cushions for a relaxed, casual vibe. Have umbrellas or large patio shades nearby for a bit of cover from the sun. No pool, no problem! Enjoy this party outdoors.

BITES

BOWLS

BOARDS

BEVERAGES

FALL

Autumn Harvest Party

- **AMBIENCE:** Taper candles; tea light candles; cozy blankets or shawls for guests. For the music, mountain folk or indie-acoustic sets the scene.
- **PRESENTATION:** Use wooden boards, ceramic bowls in earthy tones, a linen table runner, various sized pumpkins, and seasonal flowers.
- **PAIRINGS:** Highlight roasted, caramelized, spiced, sweet, and salty dishes.
- **SPACE:** Host outdoors with fall foliage, a fire pit or outdoor heater for warmth, and plenty of cozy seating.

BITES

Buffalo Chicken Meatballs *38*

Maple-Candied Bacon Deviled Eggs *61*

Red Wine Poached Pears *64*

BOWLS

Swirled Roasted Beet Whipped Feta and Maple Carrots *75*

Pumpkin Pie Dip *90*

Autumn Harvest Cobb Salad *122*

BOARDS

Simple Shop Plate *159*

Happiest Hour Plate *163*

Maple Tofu and Squash Sandwiches *194*

BEVERAGES

Grapefruit and Rosemary Fizz *213*

Dark Chocolate Tequila Espresso Martini *217*

Spiced Pomegranate Bourbon Sour *218*

Game-Day Soiree

- **AMBIENCE:** Casual, upbeat atmosphere. Have the TV playing in the background with the game on. Music here is optional, but I always like to play some of my favorite sing-along rock hits during commercial breaks.
- **PRESENTATION:** Use wooden boards, big trays, bite-size apps, flowers to match the colors of your favorite sports team, and a snack table with easy access.
- **PAIRINGS:** Highlight salty, tangy, robust, creamy, and zesty dishes.
- **SPACE:** Host indoors with ample seating space, and set up another area to mingle away from the TV.

BITES

Buffalo Chicken Meatballs *38*

Cheesy Puff Pastry Pinwheels *53*

Veggie Meatballs with Pesto *57*

BOWLS

Caramelized Onion Dip with Herbs *93*

Autumnal Goat Cheese and Squash Pasta Salad *121*

Chopped Brussels and Pecorino Salad *125*

BOARDS

Snacks for Dinner Plate *149*

Simple Shop Plate *159*

Sausage, Pepper, and Onion Focaccia Pizza *190*

BEVERAGES

The TCP *206*

Select Spritz *210*

Minty Peach Green Tea Lemonade *214*

WINTER

Ease Into the Season

- **AMBIENCE:** Cozy, warm lighting: vintage candelabras, dainty twinkle lights, and a festive Christmas tree or menorah, if applicable. This is where you rock out to your all-time favorite holiday playlist for the twentieth year in a row.
- **PRESENTATION:** Use vintage silver platters, wooden boards, velvet and gingham, and greenery and pine cones.
- **PAIRINGS:** Highlight savory, cheesy, decadent, roasted, and sweet dishes.
- **SPACE:** Host indoors by a roaring fireplace or the Yule log on the TV. Arrange seating areas with plush throw blankets and oversize pillows for extra comfort.

BITES

Savory Swiss Jammy Onion Toasts *54*

Veggie Meatballs with Pesto *57*

Red Wine Poached Pears *64*

BOWLS

Stuffed Mushroom Dip *69*

Burrata with Winter Citrus and Toasted Walnuts *107*

Chopped Brussels and Pecorino Salad *125*

BOARDS

Winter Holiday Antipasto *175*

Sausage, Pepper, and Onion Focaccia Pizza *190*

Smoked Mozzarella, Artichoke, and Pesto Focaccia Pizza *192*

BEVERAGES

Grapefruit and Rosemary Fizz *213*

Spiced Pomegranate Bourbon Sour *218*

Classic Punch Bowl *221*

Taters and 'Tinis

- **AMBIENCE:** Tea light candles, taper candles, dim lighting like a New York City bar. The music should transport you to an intimate setting with smooth soul, R&B, and classic jazz.
- **PRESENTATION:** A martini glass tower on display, colors to resemble the shades of potatoes and olives (reds, beige, greens), decorative tiered platters for serving, and greenery and baby potatoes on the tablescape.
- **PAIRINGS:** Highlight starchy, briny, cheesy, savory, and tangy dishes.
- **SPACE:** Set up a large table display with all snacks. Create a separate bar area for DIY martini garnish

BITES

BOWLS

BOARDS

BEVERAGES

Acknowledgments

Thank you to my incredible online community @ThatCheesePlate. You constantly encourage me to keep creating and evolving. Freelance life is all about the peaks and valleys, and over the years I've learned how to go with the flow, slow down, and take stock of what's important. Your support means the world.

To my family, thank you for influencing so many of these recipes, always believing in my craziest ideas, and never putting limits on what is achievable. To my friends both new and old, thank you for all of the memorable nights spent around the appetizers over the years. From the cheese parties in my New York City apartment to the snacky parties in my upstate home, you always show up with unwavering love and support. I am so lucky.

To Eve Attermann, my literary agent, thank you for believing in That Cheese Plate from day one. You've been such a cheerleader and advocate for me and I am forever grateful.

To Lisa Poe, my manager, your attention to detail, positivity, and hard work have brought That Cheese Plate to the next level over the years. Thank you for all the support.

To Amanda Englander, my editor, thank you for pushing me outside of my comfort zone. As much as I was resistant to change, you made me realize that I am, in fact, more than cheese. To Renée Bollier and Lisa Forde, thank you for your creative vision and eye.

To my photography, food-styling, and props team, Nico Schinco, Katie Wayne, Maeve Sheridan, Nikki Jessop, and Ashleigh Sarbone, thank you for introducing me to the world of cookbook shoots. Before this, I shot everything on my iPhone in my apartment, so having an actual team to help was such a game changer. Your talent and energy were so inspiring to be around. To Monica Lee for the incredible recipe testing skills and Amalia Graziani for opening the doors at Callisto Hudson Valley for us—even in the rain, it was magical. Another special thanks to Brooklyn Sour, Columbus Meats, Fresh Direct, Gourmet Sweet Botanicals, Maille, and Nuts.com for contributing to our shoot!

To many more joyful gatherings that spark a newfound sense of creativity.

With love,
Marissa

Index

NOTE: Page references in *italics* refer to photos of recipes.

D

E

F